# CHARMED BY THE SPIRIT KEEPER

One Family's Ancestral Journey

by Donna N. Webster Miles

©2019 Donna Miles

This book is a collection of information, pertaining to the author's family and friends, bound for informational purposes. The author has obtained all necessary permissions for use of maps and photos.

ISBN 978-1-7337170-4-5
(hard cover)

All rights reserved. No part of this book may be reproduced or transmitted in any form or by any means, electronic or mechanical, including photocopying, recording, or by any information storage and retrieval system, without permission in writing from the book's author or publishing agent. Contact:

Marla Jones, Book Design
(405) 354-7422

Cover Artwork: Christian Kaindl, Austria
Feather art in text: Mohamed Hassan, Ireland

Library of Congress Control Number:2019913714

## O-SI-YO

This book is dedicated to all the sacred spirits who have blessed my life.

Dewey S. Webster, my father, who shared his family legacy;

Marion Francis Webster, my brother, who inspired me to search for our lineage;

the family tribes who courageously carried the Webster gene from long gone centuries into the present with hope for our future;

and those who choose to honor me by reading this biographical memoir.

I am grateful we share this fleeting moment in time.


The Spirit Keeper

*O-SI-YO*
"All is well."

# Chapter One

Dear Ones,

Greetings of grace and peace to all.

I am writing this to everyone who has ever dreamed or pondered the probability of dancing on the heartstrings of the spirits that influence the design of who they will become. This is intended to be my personal template and hopefully a guide to all who are seekers of the mysteries that shape mortal life. I hope to be a good steward of the stories, legends, and folklore surrounding who my family, your family, has become. This is not my story. It is our story. It is a story each of us can share. Our ancestors have left meaningful blueprints that help us link the connections that distinguish who we are in the big scheme of life. It is my passion to share with you what has been passed down by those who came before me. We are blessed with the privilege to carry their baton of the past into the future.

One little, yet significant, problem I am having with this story is where to begin. For some, the answer may seem simple. You might say, "Why not begin at the beginning?" Now that makes sense. Begin at the beginning, wherever that is. Still, that presents a problem all its own as the beginning is elusive.

For several years, I have solicited the assistance of Ancestry.com to aid in the search for my sainted predecessors. Two hundred plus identities, now occupy the miniature windows on my Family Tree. My hope is to inspire each of you with images of the sacred that bring forth the spirits of all who have gone before us.

Okay, so what is it about my family, your family, that possesses me? To be specific, I am looking for closure to a story my father told when I was a child. He was a legitimate storyteller just as surely as Garrison Keillor on The Prairie Home Companion in the sixties and seventies. Much that is written here is rooted in stories belonging to him. His favorite ones were those steeped in the earthiness of the first persons who inhabited the land of our forefathers. After all, he grew up on land surrounded by the awesome Gloss (aka Glass) Mountains along the southern border of the Cimarron River once occupied by the Cheyenne/Arapaho Tribes and with the Cherokee Tribe peaked on the northern banks of the river in an area known as the Cherokee Outlet. Daddy told what I believed then was a legend linking our family with that of the Cherokee Indian Nation. Maybe his effervescent recanting of the beautiful story was so convincing I wanted it to be true. Today, I am sure it was more than a legend. It is one that has snuggled so close to the heart of fantasy that it may be difficult to sift through explicit pieces in search of factual implications. I remind you there is always at least a trace of fact in every legend. Now to authenticate this story would be nice. I am sure Daddy never dreamed he opened a real can of worms for his 'needs to know the truth' daughter. I remain driven by the provocation of the mystery of his story and who knows with a little luck I just may find a definitive answer.

What is the truth of the obscure "X" Factor in our family? What will I do if I don't find the key that unlocks this perplexity? I don't know. Psychologists might say deep in our souls we already know the answer to the dilemma we question. What will I do if I do find the answer? I don't know that either. I hope I rejoice, bask in the magic of wonder, and release the unknown to the romance of the quest. Maybe I will be driven by the innate spirits of my Native American ancestors to dance the rhythmic beat of the drum, to sing the chant of the eagle, to find peace in the serenity of the wind, to bask in the warmth of the 'Great Sun' that surrounds us and to pray to the God above and to the God of the earth for peace Oh, what a blessing.

As I have intimated, my father was born with the genetic

predisposition for story-telling. That, in itself, may explain his penchant toward our native American brothers and sisters. His was more than a fondness or predilection for the first occupants known to inhabit this great land. Early photos of our family expose the high cheek bones, broad noses, tanned, ruddy complexions, tall, erect statures, all commonalities that suggest distinct tribal connections. They are the ancestors who shared their stories of the physical and metaphysical world they knew. They believed these two worlds worked in tandem to protect and enliven the past while preserving a sacred trail toward a hopeful future.

    Storytellers connect the past with the future. Imagine our Native American friends sitting around a smoldering smoke laden fire pit basking in visions of who they were as a fearless tribe smitten with dreams of who they will become when they reclaim their greatness. Native American storytelling is steeped in tradition and reflects the resilience of the native way of being. Sacred stories and tales of small animals were the two narratives most often recanted. It was tribal custom for some to share stories only with other Indian people and were by invitation only. The invitation came through the Myth Keeper of the tribe. Consent for the request would come through The Medicine Man who would perform a scratching ceremony on the person. First, he would scratch the arm from shoulder to elbow, then elbow to wrist with a comb made of rattlesnake teeth. A red powder believed to contain healing power was blown over the red marks the comb made on the arm. Then the person was granted the privilege to hear the stories of the Myth Keeper. This was usually done in a small dome shaped earth covered hut. Often stories would go on all night. At sunrise the person would go to the water, dip himself seven times under the water while an Indian priest recited prayers. Sounds a bit like the children's story of The Little Rabbit Who Wanted Red Wings, doesn't it?

    Unlike his Native American counterparts, father waived the obligatory native custom of sharing stories only to those invited into the tent of the storyteller. Instead, he went straight for the jugular and recanted to anyone captured in his presence. He was at his best when he was reminiscing his past—the fine wine of his life. He savored its familiar flavor and allowed its fragrance to consume his whole being. With sheer delight, father accepted the role of Keeper of the Spirits in his family.

    I suppose it is fair to say that I may have inherited the Keeper gene that graced my father. Perhaps my concentration is similar to that of others in that I have a passion for guarding and preserving the spirits of those who have made a differ-ence in my life. Much of the work of those who have come before me has been to pass on wisdom learned from previous experiences, present struggles, and the spinning of dreams pointing into the future. Our Native American ancestors took advantage of the art of storytelling to entertain, to teach life lessons, to preserve traditions, to mend spirits, and to empower the souls. They were Keepers of Myth. Many of their stories were fixed in truth. Some were wrapped in the charm of folklore. In others, truth and folklore were bundled in the mythology of legend. All were recordings of tidbits of magic, of wonder, of endurance. It is with great delight I surrender all formalities that might restrict anyone from entering the tent of my forefathers to learn lessons that illuminate the soul.

    It is my hope this will inspire you to share your stories with your family, friends, and any who will listen. Everyone has a story unique to their life experiences. Some good. Some not so good. Good can be a source of healing. The impact of the not so good leaves deep, sometimes cavernous wounds. Fill the reservoir of your treasure chests with all that is good. You can't change the ill effects of the not so good. From your treasure chest of good you can withdraw the strength and courage to cope with the not so good. Healing from the not so good is possible when living in the good. Prepare to live in the good. It is important those stories be lived out and shared with others. All our lives are made richer through connecting our stories with those of others. Welcome to my stories drenched in legend, myth, folklore, and truth!

The Spirit Keeper

# Chapter Two

## O-SI-YO

  I am not sure spirits and myths get a fair shake in our twenty-first century culture. That is why I have chosen to be a Keeper of the warm and beautiful essence of the spirits of those whose footprints have marked my life. I am charged with honoring and preserving the purity of the character that is distinctly theirs.
  I think it is fair to say that Keepers of the Spirit and Keepers of the Myths have a lot in common. One actively preserves specific characteristics of another person. The other takes a more discerning approach toward discovering the truth surrounding events and happenings involving another. Both are intended to honor those who have made a significant difference in the lives of others. And both minister to yearnings of the heart.
  I was a student many years ago and I was a teacher for another number of years. That is how I know teachers make an impressionable difference in the lives of their charges.
  It is true that teachers leave indelible marks upon the lives of their students. Even though I had started sewing on my grandmother's treadle machine when I was about ten years old and maybe because of having early stitching experiences, I tackled a more difficult project in high school Home Economics class.
  In 4-H Club, with some degree of elemental success, I stitched up tea towels of all sorts, pot holders, aprons, and my

creme de la creme project was a dress made of blue and white floral feed sack fabric. Daddy bought bran as a supplement for our cows. It came in floral feed sacks. Mother collected the sacks to use for my dresses. She chose a sack with a blue and white pattern. As was our custom, she took the feed sack to the tiny grocery store in town. From a stack of sacks other women had traded in, mother found one that matched mine. She left a sack of a different color and pattern she could not use for someone who needed one that matched theirs.

The pattern I chose for my dress had a gathered waist line with a peplum over lay, a key hole neckline, and ruffled sleeves. Gathers, overlay, precision neckline, and ruffles. Big challenge for an eighth grader. I wore it in a style show at the Major County 4-H Club Fair held each year in Fairview, Oklahoma near the County Extension Office. I came home with a ribbon of some color. Proud of my gutsy fete but after all the ripping out and resewing of seams, I really didn't like the product. I remember it well.

Since my Mother didn't sew, she wanted to nurture those skills in her daughters. She always told my sister and me she would be happy to purchase any fabric we wanted to sew. Her only caveat of that declaration was that we had to wear the finished garment. When I enrolled in Home Economics as a senior in high school, the teacher's assignment was to create a structured fully lined garment. I selected a pattern for a suit with a straight skirt accentuated by a cute little short bolero jacket. Mother drove twenty-six miles to the C.R. Anthony Dry Goods Store in Fairview, Oklahoma to purchase the fabric. I chose navy blue gabardine for the exterior and a dark grey satin (the only color available) for the lining. The picture on the pattern looked smart and stylish.

I could hardly wait to begin this project. Well, darn, wouldn't you know the same thing happened as it did with the dress in 4-H Club. After ripping, taking out seams, resewing seams, putting in the zipper, taking out the zipper, interfacing the jacket, and working under the stress of time constraints, I was not so very happy with the finished product that, in the beginning, I was sure would make me look stunning and beautiful. I wore it, even took it with me to college, but it never lived up to my expectations.

Miss Couch was the Home Economics teacher. Lorraine was her given name. Fresh out of college, she had come to Seiling, Oklahoma as a first year teacher. Lorraine was a pretty dark haired young lady who exuded a sparkling personality and exuberant energy. Her dark brown eyes twinkled with delight. Her laughter was soft and gentle. Lorraine's effervescent smile was inviting and ever present. In her second year at Seiling High, she provoked Harold Stotts into relinquishing his long held title as the town's confirmed bachelor. They married in a lovely ceremony in Alva, Oklahoma.

One day after Home Economics class, when I had been struggling with the angst of sewing my infamous navy blue suit, Mrs. Stotts asked me to step into her office. In a soft direct voice, she talked of my frustrations with sewing. She reminded me I had chosen a difficult project, one that at times challenged my sewing skills. Then she spoke words I will never forget. She said, "Donna you are a beautiful young lady. You know the techniques of sewing. You have a lovely voice, you always have a smile for everyone, you can do anything you set your mind to. You do not have to be like anybody else. Just be you."

Lorraine magnified my identity by reminding me of my innate worthiness. I remember her loving serenity and her compassionate wisdom. She was speaking to the Christ Follower spirit taking up residence within my young life. My heart grieved when a few short years after I left school, she was diagnosed with cancer and died.

Sometime later, in one of my darkest hours, when it seemed I'd lost my way, I heard her repeat those words of encouragement and love. Everyone needs someone, perhaps a spirit, whose whispers of affirmation reverberate through their very being reminding them they are okay, they have a right to be here in this lifetime, and they are worthy of love. Her words remain like money stored in my memory bank. I have the luxury of taking them out when I feel wounded by the world. They comfort me and refresh my belief in who I am and who I want to be. Her spirit continues to guide me.

I am the Keeper of Lorraine's Spirit and all the other Lorraine's who have supported me, believed in me, and loved me.

There is a spirit that lives within each of us. Lorraine and I share a common spirit.

Here are my words to you as you travel along this journey called life. Summon together a tribe of fellow travelers who exude quiet serenity. A gathering of those who ponder the meaning of existence in this sometimes strange world. Those who feel obliged to remind you of the spirit that lives within your soul. Garner a tribe that espouses integrity, compassion, and love. And ones who will honor your stories in the most holy and sacred niche of their hearts.

I am a Keeper of the myths of my ancestors whose rose-colored aesthetics have enhanced the quality of life for all on whose shoulders I stand.

For now, here is what I have learned about my family, as well as the Cherokee Nation's occupation of the Cherokee Outlet on the northern banks of the Cimarron River in Woods County, Oklahoma and the Cheyenne/Arapaho Tribes who took up residence in the valley cutting through the Gloss Mountains on the southern banks of the Cimarron in Major County, Oklahoma.

Photo by Steddon Sikes

# Gloss Mountains
# Northwestern Oklahoma

# Chapter Three

*O-SI-YO*

    An air of sacredness hung over her as she made her way through the mountain range of eastern Illinois. The gentle rhythmic clip clop of her paint pony could be heard above the stillness of the towering red pine forming a canopy over the trail she followed. Her serene buckskin-clothed body staunch with resignation straddled the bareback of her paint pony while her long raven braid swayed with indifference to his cadence. Her right hand clutched the mane of her mount to give directions; in her left, she held a swaddled bundle. She rode with confidence and determination as she made her way in and around and through the winding string of twists and turns. It was believed this Indian Maiden was of the Cherokee Indian tribe.

    This story became the X Factor in the Webster family waiting for truth and light.

# Chapter Four

## O-SI-YO

    Did you ever wonder what Christopher Columbus expected to find when he arrived on the eastern seaboard of America October 12 of 1492? History teaches that he was the first to discover and to explore America. Now that which once was believed fact has come into question. Some believe the expedition of Hernando de Soto in 1542, was the first contact between southeastern American Indians and Europeans. He conducted expeditions through the southeastern United States and came in contact with three Cherokee villages. Others said it was Marco Polo in 1740 who was first to arrive on the shores of the North American continent. Perhaps it was the Chinese who traipsed through the mountains and valleys of this new land in search of human inhabitants? Or, even the Vikings led by Leif Erickson who first stepped on the shores of this northern continent.

    Even so, it was thought that in 1673 Hernando de Soto, introduced English immigrants to the art of trading with the tribes. By about 1711, the English were in the business of trading guns to the Cherokees in exchange for their help in fighting the Tuscarora Tribe. Then around 1740, the Cherokee began transitioning to a commercial hunting and farming lifestyle.

    Still, Columbus was considered among the first to arrive on the scene. His voyages are credited with influencing European relations with America through exploration and colonization. He made significant contributions in the historical development of who the nation has become.

In 1775, one Cherokee village was described as having one hundred houses, each with a garden, orchard, hothouse, and hog pens. After the war with the colonists, the Cherokees signed a peace treaty in 1785. Then by the early 1800s, most of the Cherokee had adopted a farming lifestyle similar to that of the European immigrants.

This story is rooted in the lives of those first people who occupied parts of the Smoky Mountains in North Carolina, South Carolina, Alabama, Tennessee, and Georgia centuries ago. Over the years, many have attempted to determine the specific origin of these first settlers. Much research has been conducted to unlock the mysterious identity of those considered the first Americans. That debate has never been resolved. In his expeditions, Columbus discovered and recorded the activities of people clustered in communities and living in earthy huts nestled in the mountains of states now known as North and South Carolina, Georgia, Tennessee and as far south as Louisiana. He believed them to be the indigenous Spiro Mound builders of 500 to 1300 A.D. Columbus concluded these solemn people were the Native Americans of this vast country and were identifiable as tribal Indians.

I can only imagine what Columbus must have thought the first time he came upon a village inhabited by people of titian skin and hair as black as night going about their daily routines of caring for the crops in their fields. A primary intent of Co-lumbus was to spread Christianity in what he believed to be a primitive sector of the world, occupied by pagan, unprincipled, idolatrous creatures void of faith in a supreme being. He must have been pleasantly surprised to find that he had stumbled upon communities of hard working people who valued the natural order of nature. They were people who paid tribute to the sun and moon as sources of strength and direction. To Native Americans, religious spirituality is integrated into every aspect of the fabric of their lives. Each Indian tribe respects the integrity, sacred value, and inherent privacy of religious practices of others. They practice the art of silence especially when in uncomfortable circumstances. For them, it is a matter of self-preservation. Speak when you have something meaningful to communicate. Some of the rest of us, could learn from this. Sometimes others interpret their quietness as indifference when, in reality it is a deeply embedded form of respectful personal etiquette. Native Americans exercise patience. It is a survival virtue that supports their belief that all things unfold in their own time and that attempts to disrupt the spontaneous progression diminishes the targeted effect. In the Indian world, seeing and listening are seasoned skills. Storytelling, oral communication, experiential and observational learning are methods for transferring knowledge.

After spending time with these quiet, gentle people, Columbus concluded that these were indeed the first dwellers of the new world and as such deserved to be honored for their vigilant stewardship of this bounteous land called America. Not all people who landed on the shores of uncharted territory held the same reverence for those who were established residents.

White European explorers, who encroached upon Indian territories, disturbed the balance of food and environmental resources. The introduction of horses into the tribes transformed the Plains Indians from foot nomads into horse fanciers. In the beginning, the Indians believed the horse was manna from heaven for their culture. Later, they would consider the horse a two-edged sword destabilizing, dispossessing, and detrimental to their population. While it aided them in moving, hunting, trading and fighting, it led to the destruction of their quiet, gentle, peaceful way of being.

New settlers who followed Christopher Columbus, Leif Erickson, Coronado, a Spanish conquistador, and many other newcomers lusted over the lands the Indians had developed on reservations they called home. The Cherokee nation was a tangential target when gold was discovered in the imposing mountains of the Carolinas, Tennessee and as far south as Alabama. Thus the Federal Government began to argue the case for taking the land from this innocent and generous people.

I think of that song that goes something like this: "Go ahead and cheat your neighbor, go ahead and cheat your friend. Do it in the name of freedom. You can justify it in the end................." And this is what happened to the quiet brave red man who mustered the courage to blaze a trail into the unknown wilderness of the Great Smoky Mountains along the eastern seaboard of what is known as the United States of America. He assumed command and stood sentry to protect and preserve all that surrounded him. Then, with grace and dignity, he forfeited it to another people.

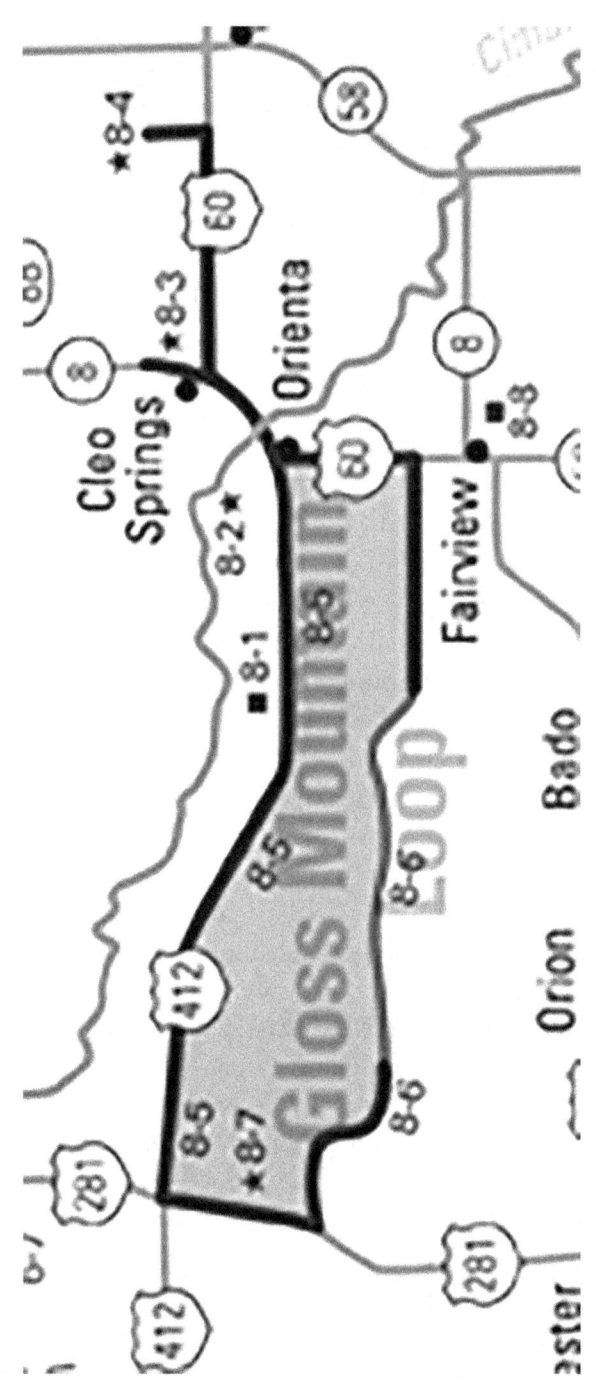

In the early 1800's, the United States Government forced the Cheyenne Indians to move to Indian Territory in Oklahoma. Some were not happy about this arrangement and some decided to flee to Montana. Another faction decided to locate in the Great Plains of Oklahoma along the lackadaisical Cimarron River. Those who chose to migrate to Montana were the Northern Cheyennes and lived on reservations. The ones staying in Oklahoma settled on government trust lands and were known as the Southern Cheyennes. A not so small band led by Chief Dull Knife decided to settle along the southern banks of the Cimarron River in the heart of the Gloss Mountains in Major County, Oklahoma. In the move west, the Cheyenne linked up with the Arapaho Tribe. Today they are known as the Cheyenne-Arapaho Indian Tribe. In the end, the federal government carved out a reservation for these two tribes in the vicinity of Canton, Oklahoma. Many remain in that area today.

A bounty of bison grazed on the abundance of tall grassland insuring a good food supply. The Cimarron guaranteed a plentiful water source, and the tall, rugged, glistening red mountains confirmed the territorial boundaries. Soon cone-like tents dotted the river banks and the Cheyenne settled into what they hoped would be a life of peaceful contentment.

Chief Dull Knife of the Cheyenne's traveled north into the watershed area of the Cimarron Basin and crossed the River. The tribe called themselves "Tsis tsis'tas" (Tse-TSES-tas) which means "the beautiful people." The area became known as Cheyenne Valley, Indian Territory. Some Cheyenne-Arapaho strayed in and around small towns in Dewey County, Oklahoma. I remember seeing them sitting in recessed doorways, wrapped in their traditional blankets along the streets of Seiling, Oklahoma.

I can't explain the optimism of the Cheyenne/Arapaho because surely by this time in history the great Indian chiefs had learned the cruel lesson that life never remains the same and that contentment comes at a price. Maybe it is innate in the native American spirit to presume the goodness of man prevails.

Then again, there was this Chief Dull Knife. Yes, that really was his name. He may or may not have assessed the circumstances accurately but he was up against odds that would cause most people to throw in the towel. After Custer's defeat at the Battle of the Little Big Horn, his cavalry attacked Dull Knife's camp on the "Powder River." Most of Dull Knife's Tribe escaped but their camp and possessions were destroyed. Dull Knife surrendered to the Army. He and his tribe was sent to a reservation in Indian Territory, Oklahoma. The Cheyenne reservation was located in northern Oklahoma bordered on the south by the Gloss Mountain range and with the Cimarron River on the north. They protested that the land was not productive, the climate unhealthy; many in the Tribe died. Dull Knife joined forces with Chief Little Wolf of the northern Cheyennes. On September 9, 1878, they led what was left of Dull Knife's tribe, eighty-nine warriors and two hundred forty-six women and children, from their reservation in the valley of the Cheyenne. They traveled more than 400 miles, defeating and eluding the Army's efforts to return them to the reservation. More than 10,000 soldiers were dispatched to bring the tribe back to the Cheyenne Reservation. Finally, Lone Wolf and Dull Knife separated (Lone Wolf's band surrendered to the Army and was allowed to remain in Montana). Dull Knife and his people hoped to take refuge through the Red Cloud Agency only to find the agency had been shut down. The Tribe surrendered peaceably to the Army and was imprisoned. Once again, the military tried to force the Tribe to return to Oklahoma. They tried to starve them into submission. The Tribe broke out of prison and made a desperate attempt to escape. Several were killed and some were recaptured. Chief Dull Knife and six of his family members made it to the safety of the Pine Ridge Reservation. By then, public opinion was on the side of the Indians and the government had to abandon plans to relocate them. Dull Knife and his people (fewer than 80) were placed on the reservation with Lone Wolf and his northern Cheyennes near the Tongue and Rosebud rivers in Montana.

At the time the Cheyennes occupied the reservation along the Cimarron River in Major County, Oklahoma, there were all kinds of skirmishes between the Tribe, the white settlers in the valley, and the persevering cattle drivers. We mustn't forget the Dalton Gang of criminals and other robbers who took refuge in the caves tucked under the crevices of the Gloss Mountains. Most were mean without reason and killed for sport.

    Much of this story culminates in and around the Gloss Mountains in northern Oklahoma and more specific to the Webster Ranch located on the banks of the Cimarron River in Major County, Oklahoma in the valley of the Cheyenne.

# Chapter Five

## O-SI-YO

Intense heat sucked all but a tender breeze from the air. The leaves on the elms in our yard swayed in the occasional whispered puffs of wind. In the heavy stillness, I became aware of a steady, rhythmic beat from far away. Mother opened the screen door and stepped out on the porch. On this day, she was canning peaches. The heat from the cookstove in the kitchen intensified the discomfort of the day. In a few short moments, she too, became aware of the sounds. "Do you hear that, Mother? What is it?" I asked.

Mother listened for an instant then replied, "I think the Cheyenne/Arapaho are Pow Wowing this week."

Every September the tribe came from near and far to sing, dance, and tell stories. They set up teepees and made camp in old man Brown's field where the ponies and greyhounds used to run. The origin of the Cheyenne/Arapaho Pow Wows was that of a traditional spiritual experience that started many years ago.

Teepees sprang up like mole hills in dry desert grass. Dust fogged the newly defined roads as vehicles transported revelers with all their elaborate regalia to the tribal party. At dusk, they emerged, like moths from a cocoon, clothed in color-ful ancestral garb, with all the accoutrements of feathers and fur. They prepared for their transformation from the worldly mundane to the sacred and terrestrial. The gentle rhythmic beat of tribal drums, the lilting songs of the flute mesmerized their hungry hearts toward a time when they were a nation aligned with the earth. This was the hope in a Pow Wow. It was the Indian Sun Dance, a ceremony where there was feasting, singing, and dancing, a conference among Native Americans. A time of celebration with friends, some they had seen the year before, some they hadn't seen in several years. They shared stories, played games, cooked over an open fire, and yes, with toes a-twitter they danced. I suspect it was an event something like a family reunion where they came together to reminisce about times past and dream about the future.

It was a time when the tribe would retreat from the world and immerse themselves in the spiritual traditions of their ancestors. An opportunity to see ones they had not seen in a long time, to revive friendships, to share stories of their past and present, and to pass a cup of peace. Cheyenne Pow Wows were called Indian Sun Dances. They chose the right place when they selected Seiling, Oklahoma for their annual celebration. No scarcity of sun in September in northwest Oklahoma.

They rid themselves of twentieth century attire, donned their tribal raiments, in an effort to experience the lifestyle of those who had gone before them. Children and adults played all kinds of games. Contests were held to determine who had created the most authentic native garb or who had finessed the skill of performing specific dance routines. More than likely, there was a display of art work, painting, weaving, sculpture, and beading. It was a time laced with magic and wonder.          Did you know that Pow Wow means 'he dreams?' Since I have never been invited to a Pow Wow, I can only imagine that it might be like a spiritual experience where people drop inhibitions in their quest to experience serenity in a oneness with God. Each year many tribes, from around the nation, converge on Oklahoma City to participate in the Red Earth Festival, the premier of all Pow Wows.

The Cheyenne believe in a supreme being as the creator of life. They embrace the wise one above as the God who lives in the earth. Perhaps the Pow Wow is somewhat like the more familiar experiences of meditation where we quiet ouselves to give God a chance to talk to us. Could it be that Native Americans implore the use of the drums, and music, and dance to make loud their call to God?

In my feeble attempts to understand Cheyenne spiritual beliefs, I reference a reassuring tenet of my faith to invite God into my presence. My precept is "Be Still and Know That I Am God." Today, as I hear the exaggerated beating of the drums and the vocal supplications of the Cheyenne/Arapaho calling the tribe to engage in a personal spiritual journey, I wonder if their mantra might be something like, 'Make loud and call God into our midst.' It may be a Pow Wow, in some ways, replicates the old fashioned tent revival where the soul is nourished in anticipation and hope of being set free.

The Cheyenne tended to be more nomadic than some other tribes. They were sedentary, agricultural Indians who located in northern Oklahoma along the southern banks of the Cimarron, wrapped in the mystique of the Gloss Mountains in Woods and Major Counties. In Oklahoma, they abandoned their sedentary lifestyle for that of a Plains Horse culture tribe hunting buffalo.

# Chapter Six

Cone Marker-Indian Medicine Wheel
Northwestern University

It was common for Native American Tribes to build markers in obvious places to proclaim to those who followed which tribe had gone before them. I suppose, these might be compared to road signs. One of my father's favorite stories was of a marker found on top of a bluff in the Gloss Mountains in Cheyenne Valley where he grew up. More than likely, the Cheyenne/Arapaho built it when they occupied the valley. It was a cone-like marker built of the red clay of the mountains perhaps to declare to other tribes that the Cheyennes had gone through the territory along the Cimarron River in Indian Territory. The marker was discovered by our Webster family who lived in Cheyenne Valley in the early 1900's. Once upon a time, many markers dotted the landscape of Oklahoma. In our father's storytelling, with a great deal of pride and drama, he would point toward the top of the mountain where the marker was standing and repeat the historical tidbit of the significance of the marker. We looked on in awe and perhaps with a little skepticism. Sometime in the 1950's, the marker disappeared. After searching for its whereabouts, we learned it had been taken down by Northwestern Oklahoma State University in Alva, Oklahoma for research purposes. I suspect it is possible the red clay like structure crumbled into an irreparable state never to be seen again.

Father had repeated his stories of the native Americans who lived in Cheyenne Valley, but the reality escaped us until we were older. We were too inexperienced to distinguish fact from fiction.

# Chapter Seven

## O-SI-YO

Legend had it that a courageous young Cherokee maiden was the mother of the infant she carried. Others believed she was my great grandmother and the infant my grandmother. I have attempted to trace the authenticity of the story. I'm not sure it can be traced if all ties to the Cherokee Tribe were severed.

The year was 1838, twenty-five years after an edict issued by President Andrew Jackson forced the Cherokee Tribe on one of the saddest journeys recorded in the history of our country. Removed from their territory and herded across the nation like the buffalo they hunted, the gentle, innocent red men were stripped of their pride and courage. They were forced to walk two hundred some grueling days to what was to be a promised territory but to what turned out to be a barren land with little resources for survival. Many died along the way. The bloodstained trail of the Cherokee Nation was known as the Trail of Tears.

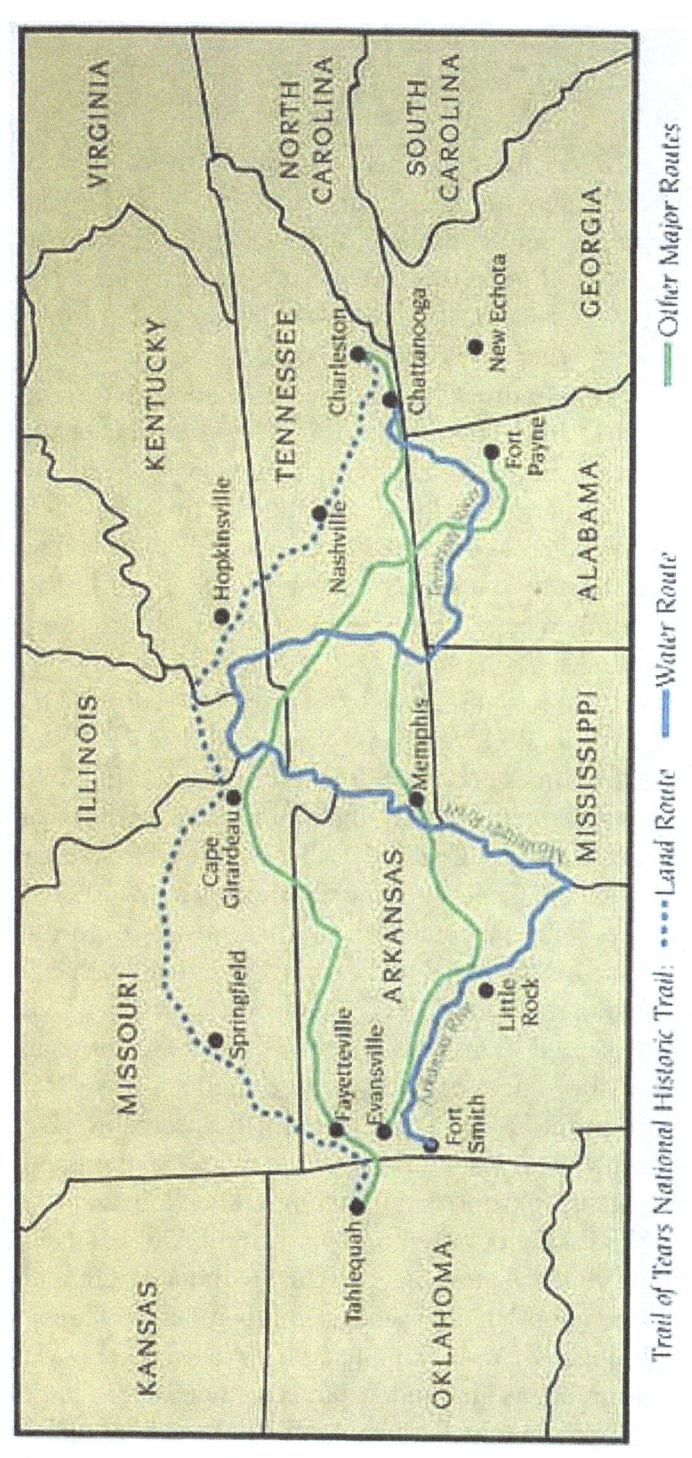

Courtesy of the U.S. National Park Service and Cherokee National Historical Society

# O-SI-YO

The Cherokee Native American Indian tribe, one of the largest tribes settled in the country, had lived in Georgia, Tennessee, North and South Carolina, Alabama, and Louisiana for many years. They lived in cabins rather than customary tee pees. Like the Cheyenne/Arapaho, they were a religious and spiritual people. They were eager to fit into the fabric of the nation. In the 1800's, they began to dress like the white man, assumed some of his farming ways, and even accepted the intermarriage of the two ethnicities. In Tennessee, many lived in what is called the Qualla Boundary. There were those who thought this area was a Reservation for the Cherokee Native American Tribe. In reality, it was a Land Trust under the supervision of the Bureau of Indian Affairs and was home to large numbers of Cherokees. It was some eighty-two square miles in size.

In 1828, gold was discovered on Cherokee land. The greediness of the Federal Government compelled it to force the Indians out of their homes and to settle in other places. In 1830, President Andrew Jackson put in place the Indian Remov-al Act that demanded Indians of the Five Civilized Tribes be moved from their home land. In 1831, the Choctaw Tribe was the first to be ushered out. This was the Tribe that suffered the most deaths from the repercussions of the historic Trail of Tears in 1838 to 1839. Next, in 1832, the Seminole Tribe was forced to leave. Then in 1834, the Creek Nation set out to discover Indian Territory, Oklahoma. The Chickasaw Tribe joined the weary band of humanity in 1837. The Cherokees were the last hold out. In 1838, they were forced to abandon all their belongings and to march, yes march, a thousand miles to a foreign land appropriated for them in Oklahoma.

What kind of a deal is that? Just think of it, a land half way across the United States. I feel certain the Indians were sold a real shoddy 'bill of goods' in this exchange for their peaceful home in the Smoky Mountains. And to top that, Henry Ford had not yet invented the automobile. That didn't happen until 1908. They were forced to 'march' on foot. Yes, on foot. With leather buffalo hide moccasins as shoes, garbed in long skirts of heavy material, and bodies draped in blankets woven of fur sacrificed by animals on the run. They trudged on foot from Tennessee, Georgia, and North and South Carolina to a far away dismal, uninhabited land President Andrew Jackson proclaimed as Indian Territory.

Dense fog hung heavy over the Great Smoky Mountains blanketing the hallows in abominable darkness. Earth's retaliation to man's despicable evil conspiracy against the innocent of its kind. In the strangling silence, gut wrenching despair reached into its soul, coating the landscape with a retch of sadness. No antidote to heal the pain. The dye was cast that would forever stain the fabric of America. It was a Trail of Tears winding its way along the rivers and trails and foothills of Tennessee, the Carolinas, Georgia destined for a promised land in Oklahoma Indian Territory.

The Qualla Boundary Indian Reservation, nestled in the midst of the tall and majestic hemlock trees in the heart of the sacred Smoky Mountains near Gatlinburg, Tennessee was home to the eastern Cherokee Tribe. Approximately thirteen hundred acres of land had been inhabited by the red man and, according to some historians, forever or at least, since the 1700's. Little by little the United States government imposed upon the land south of the Hiawassee and the Tennessee Rivers. Under the provisions of an 1830 law, land grants were made on Cherokee land in middle and eastern Tennessee. The law authorized grants to land on the north and east of the established boundaries of the reservation. In the early 1800's, wayside settlements sprang up along the outside borders of the shrinking Reservation.

The Treaty of New Echota, was put forth by President Andrew Jackson. This was also known as the Treaty of Removal. It was signed in 1836 with the Cherokee nation and allowed for the expulsion of the Cherokee people from the Ocoee District in Georgia. The United States Government promised the Cherokee Nation $5,000,000 in return for their land but it was never paid. Never, as in not ever, as in not to this day in 2017 has this debt been paid. Senator Daniel Webster, 1782-1852 (not sure if there is a relationship to our Webster family) was a noted orator and humanitarian and a member of the Whig Party (later became the

Republican Party) who was appointed in 1836 by Presidents William Henry Harrison, John Tyler, and Millard Fillmore as Secretary of State, who fought to stop this government action against the Native Americans but was not successful. I think it is fair to say that most of us in our Webster family would claim him related or not.

# Chapter Eight

O-SI-YO

On the morning of May 23, 1838, the removal of the Cherokees began. Troops were sent in to round up all Cherokees who had not voluntarily complied with the edict of removal. The helpless Cherokees were arrested, dragged from their homes, driven by bayonet point into stockades (concentration camps) until such time the government could forcibly move them to land chosen as the new home for the tribe. Their homes were burned, property destroyed. Masses mobilizing and trudging along the fog laden foothill trails of the Smokies. Away from their beloved reservations, a ponderous flood of humanity.
A young couple living near the edge of the Qualla Indian Reservation were witness to the brutality that was happening. Thomas Widger of the Choctaw Indian Tribe and his wife Sarah Elizabeth Smith Widger kept a despairing eye on the sad Cherokee as they trekked along the trail near the outskirts of Gatlinburg, Tennessee just beyond their quaint little cottage. Sarah Elizabeth Smith Widger's heritage resided in Transylvania, Romania. She was both shocked and dismayed by the atrocious scene unfolding in the once peaceful territory of America. For the moment, they kept vigil from their

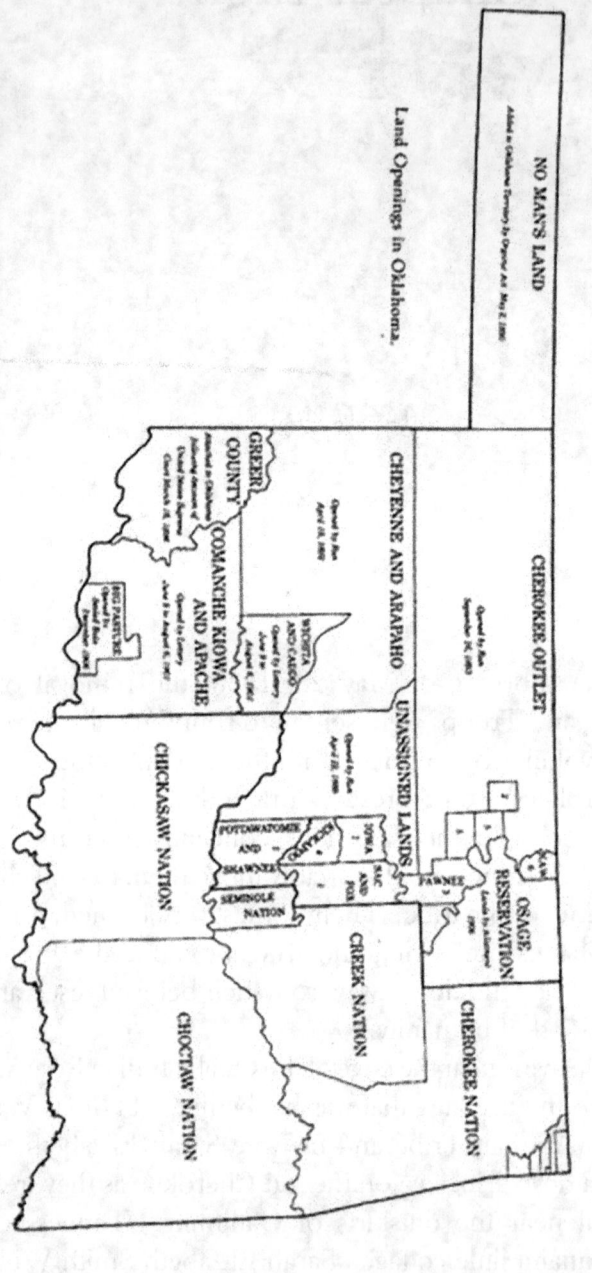

Indian Territory, 1889

Courtesy of the Oklahoma Historical Society

weathered, rustic porch.

In resolute unity, Thomas and Sarah extended sympathy to family and friends as they journeyed onward. They questioned: Should they go with them or should they stay behind? Making their decision more difficult was the fact that Sarah was a few months with child. If it happened to be a girl baby they would name her Sidney Ellen. Even so, as the pain invaded their consciences, their decision became obvious. Thomas walked the short path to the lot where the horses were kept. He bridled one for himself and one for Sarah. Then led them to the porch in front of their modest cabin.

Dressed in buckskin, the rich color of the caramel of her skin and with three regal eagle feather's affixed near the top of the tight black braid swaying down her back, there was a certain royal ambience about her. When Sarah explained to her parents their plans to join in this sad movement her english language was refined and unbroken. The fluidity of her tender voice accentuated the serenity of her solemn, gentle smile. Never before had Thomas seen anyone as beautiful. When she rested her kind brown eyes on him, his blood ran warm like honey in the sun. He was smitten by her presence. Thomas watched as Sarah climbed astride her steed. She shuffled to settle into a comfortable position. Then she gave a gentle tug on the bridle that directed her horse to begin the long journey toward a place called Indian Territory, Oklahoma. Thomas mounted his horse, adjusted the saddle bags containing their meager belongings, pulled on the reins of his horse and fell in line behind Sarah. They had a deep sense that they were leaving the only home they had ever known. It was a time when faith bridled indignation, released surreal determination, and strengthened the power of free will. Then Thomas and Sarah rode into the unknown.

# Chapter Nine

*O-SI-YO*

The Cherokees were divided into several inordinate categories. The first detachment was ordered to travel by water to Indian Territory. They set out on June 6, 1838 and followed the Tennessee River. Some traveled on open barges. Others hopped steamboats leaving from Ross Landing in Kentucky, then on to the Ohio, and continued the remainder of their journey on the Arkansas River that carried them into Indian Territory on June 19, 1838.

The next was a land detachment. Government military troops forced the Indians to leave all their belongings behind and set off on foot or horseback. Some were fortunate enough to have wagons to carry family and staples. Their travels start-ed in Tennessee then to southwest Kentucky, and southern Illinois. After crossing the Mississippi River they trekked across southern Missouri into the northwest corner of Arkansas. Most likely this is the route my Webster family took.

They clung to the winding trails of the Smoky Mountains of Tennessee in sad pursuit of a promised land called Indian Territory, Oklahoma. Without maps to navigate their way or to give them an inkling of an idea how long the journey was, it would seem preposterous to assume they could conceptualize the immensity of the task before them. Like cattle and sheep they were driven in colossal herds. Each detachment was accompanied by a Conductor, an assistant Conductor, an Administrator of the United States Army, a Physician, and a Clergy.

The distinct rhythmic cadence of their staunch laborious advance galvanized a tempo that resonated decibels of fury and indignation. A thunderous fusion of the penalties imposed on the dignity of their existence against the cries of perseverance and despair. In the beginning, the ear had to search for the oncoming intrusion. Then the collective thunderous clanking of hooves against mountain rocks, paraphernalia adjustments, and thousands of faint yet audible voices broadcast the obvious invasion. Like an army they threaded their way in and around the mountain trails. Sometimes loud and stormy; other times mute and eerie, a mysterious murky vapor of suppressed anger veiled the masses on the move. The proud Cherokee were on a journey into the unknown. A journey that would be recorded as one of the worst blights on the history of governance of the United States of America.

On a cold October morning, the sky laden with dark gray nimbus clouds signaled winter was nipping at their heels. A cold drizzle masked the hemlock and chilled to the bone those who suffered persecution. They were loaded onto 645 wagons to facilitate their continued movement westward. On November 17, 1838, a terrific sleet and snow storm befell the sufferings of the Cherokees. They had to sleep in wagons, and some slept on the ground with no fire to give them relief from the cold. Some 4,000 of the 16,000 died from exposure, starvation, and disease. They were forced to begin the one thousand mile trek to Indian Territory in Oklahoma. They were not allowed to go into any towns or villages along the way, making the trip longer and more punishing as they were made to maneuver the long way around towns. Many walked on foot, others were allowed to take canoes, or wagons, and some were fortunate to travel on horseback. Men, women, children died. Some spoke of this event using Cherokee language and called it Nu nada ul tsun yi — The Place Where They Cried. Historians record quite the opposite. They say they marched in silence.

# Quallah Boundary
Home of the Eastern Cherokee Indians
Photo by: Kevin Brocious

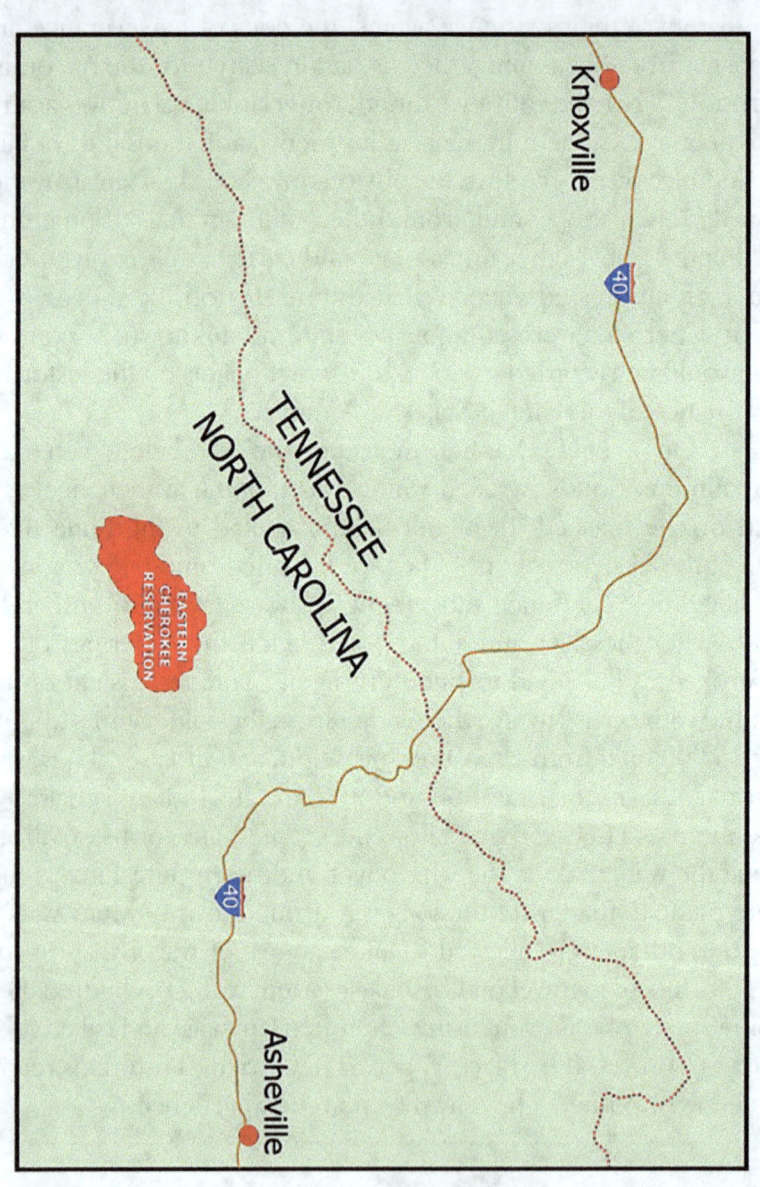

# Chapter Ten

O-SI-YO

    The proud Cherokee were a weary, sad, innocent people as they wound their way along the narrow trails of the sacred mountains of Tennessee and on the banks of rushing rivers toward Illinois and a promised land in Oklahoma Indian Territory. They walked with heavy, disillusioned hearts. Their fateful journey ended on March 26th, 1839. Most of those remaining arrived in Oklahoma near Westerville. They camped along the Illinois River near Tahlequah.
    One soldier who was forced to participate in this violation of human assault said "....the Cherokee Removal was the cruelest work I ever knew."
    What comes to my mind as I reflect on this time is an event that happened in my lifetime. It began April 9th, 1942 during World War II. The Japanese Imperial Army imposed the 'Bataan Death March' upon the Prisoners Of War it held in captivity. Around 90,000 to 100,000 American and Filipino prisoners were forced to make a sixty-five mile grueling march from Mariveles to the southern Bataan Peninsula to San Fernando. The walk took five days. Thousands died from brutality, starvation, disease, beatings, bayonetings, and murder.
    Man's inhumanity towards man makes countless thousands mourn. It would seem lessons taught are so many times repeated.

Society just doesn't get it. Perhaps they would if they held the spirits of those who suffered the torturous treat-ment.

One writer reflects: "The Cherokee did everything they were asked to except one thing. They couldn't abdicate who they were. The fact they were Cherokee was against them. They carried with them all that was Cherokee. They were Christian, they were literate, they had a government much like ours, but ultimately they were Indians. In the end, being Indian is what killed them."

I wonder if the Cherokees were so weary from their arduous journey west they dropped what was left of their belongings and made their claim in the immediate vicinity of Indian Territory. It was an area about forty miles inside the eastern border of the State of Oklahoma and became known as Tahlequah. Now it is the official Tribal head quarters of the Cherokees.

In the late 1880's, a Tribe of brave Cherokee chose to move on west to the central part of the state. They must have decided to follow the Cimarron River. When they reached the beautiful Gloss Mountains, embellished by super abundant prairie grass where the magnificent buffalo roamed in Major and Woods Counties, Oklahoma, they pitched their tents and prepared to live in the freedom of the unassigned lands. Upon their arrival and to their surprise, they discovered the Cheyenne/Arapaho had chosen the same area for encampment. The two factions had difficulty sharing the bountiful water of the river, the lush prairie grass, and the plentiful food supply of buffalo. The federal government stepped in to arbitrate. It declared the valley area winding through the Gloss Mountains on the southern banks of the Cimarron River would belong to the Cheyenne. That became known as Cheyenne Valley. Land north of the river was appropriated for the Cherokee and was called The Cherokee Outlet.

My Webster family pulled up stakes and left Tennessee between 1825-1845. Some lived through this tragic historical Native American movement. Thanks to them, I have a passionate appreciation for the historic Tribal families who trudged along the gruesome Trail of Tears to claim a homeland. In 1912, my grandfather, Marion Francis Webster I, homesteaded along the banks of the Cimarron River in Major County, Oklahoma on land previously occupied by remnants of the Cherokee Tribe on the north of the river and the Cheyenne-Arapaho on the south.

# Chapter Eleven

*O-SI-YO*

My father, Dewey Webster, was born in 1898, a middle child in a family of 14 children. Eleven survived the birthing. A financially poor family; a family rich in passion and grit. He was a keeper of their family spirit and it is my hope to con-tribute to his legacy. Mother was born in 1908. Her birth certificate reads born in Indian Territory, Oklahoma. Even though statehood was declared in 1907, one might suspect that the official paperwork was not filed until sometime later.

Father's imposing six foot plus figure exuded confidence and determination. His stately frame accentuated his somewhat calculating and commanding presence. He was a barber by profession, a self anointed farmer who drew strength from earthy solitude, a musician whose thirsty soul drank from the cup of lyrical and rhythmical syncopations. Father could play multiple instruments. His instrument of choice was a violin. With pride he used the term 'fiddle' to identify his magical strings.

Most of the 11 Webster children had a specific instrument. My mother's side of the family had to create instruments from the kitchen when they gathered. Mother or Aunt Edna played the piano. Others would grab anything from a roasting pan, a skillet, the old wash board, numerous wooden spoons and beguile the birth of euphoric rhythms.

As I have said, father was a self proclaimed storyteller who thrived on sharing stories. His dominate self went on exhibition when he was behind the wheel of the family's old 1933 Ford sedan. Then he became the alter persona of Clifton Webb in the 1950 movie, Cheaper By The Dozen. Webb played the role of a stiff, precise, stringent, pristine father of twelve children who governed the life of his family with emphatic confidence and indisputable expectations. Jeanne Crain, Webb's counterpart, and Irene, my mother, portrayed the equalizers of the family.

Father rescued our pre-owned 1933 Ford sedan from Mr. Ezell. The car was seasoned by years of faithful service. Sometimes its performance depended on the erratic Oklahoma weather. We had no garage for Ol' Betsy (the name Father had given the car). In the winter, she suffered from a sluggish engine. Like many cars in the thirties Ol' Betsy was black. She kept vigil parked outside the kitchen door of our four room white stucco bungalow.

Betsy had one peculiarity that made me uncomfortable. When driving along pitch black country roads at night, suddenly her lights would yield to the darkness leaving father searching the boundaries of the ditches outlining our way. That usually meant the tiny round fuse located under the base of the steering wheel was not making a good connection. Father would pull over to what he hoped was the side of the road and ask, "Does anyone have any chewing gum?" Someone was sure to come up with a gum wrapper. Sticks of Juicy Fruit or Double Mint gum were wrapped in a thin foil covering. Feeling for the fuse in the dark, Father would finally pull it out, wrap the foil around it, place it back in the tiny slot where it belonged and once again the connection was good and we had lights.

Since Betsy was our only mode of transportation, everyone in the family learned to make haste to get on board when father turned the key in the ignition for fear they might be destined to spend the afternoon home alone. Walking into town or to visit relatives thirty to fifty miles away was not a viable option.

Four door cars in the thirties were equipped with bench seats making it possible to carry three passengers in the front and three in the back. No seat belts in those days. Father positioned himself behind the steering wheel. Mother took her place on the passenger side and we kids took turns riding up front with our parents. My two brothers and I scrambled for choice window seats in the back. When all the dust settled and everyone reconciled their place in the car, father put the car in gear and pressed on the accelerator.

Highway 281 was a dirt road that stretched in front of our farm. There were few hard surfaced roads in our part of northwest Oklahoma. Anytime we set out on a trek, be it long or short, we first took to the loamy highway that connected with another sand or clay covered road. The threadbare tires on the car spun a few times searching for traction in the hot sand of highway 281 when father made the left hand turn toward Griever Canyon and Bouse Junction. Heat from the early morning sun beat down on the car. Air conditioning was four open windows, multiple gaping holes in the weather worn roof of the car, and numerous vents between the floorboards. Barring a flat tire or some other unforeseen malfunction, the thirty mile drive to our grandparents ranch in the Valley of the Cheyenne was a mere sixty minutes. On dirt based roads, with ruts sometimes hub cap deep, the speedometer rarely clocked more than forty-five miles an hour. The floor board in the back seat sported mini open caverns that exposed the sand and clay of the road. On occasion when father hit high center with the car, a spray of sand erupted through the floor vents like a fizzling Fourth of July firecracker. Other times, in a matter of moments following heavy rainfalls, those eruptions were like miniature red geysers that purled up and pooled around our feet as father maneuvered the car through the muddy waters. Today, this would give me a dreadful anxiety attack allowing for the danger involved. But in this time and place we did what we had to do with what we had. None of us was frightened or hurt. An angel on patrol was watching out for us.

Sunday was deemed our day of rest. No movies. No shopping at Walmart. (There was no Walmart, only Rothenberger's and Branstetter's Groceries and they were closed on Sundays). No working in the fields. The day was dedicated to attending worship services at the Methodist Church. By some magic, I'll never know how she did it, mother always managed to have a dinner of fried chicken or a succulent roast, complete with creamy mashed potatoes, peas, strawberry jello with bananas, and cake or pie waiting for us when we returned from services. After lunch, my sister and I served on KP duty in the kitchen while our parents took a much deserved nap. Somewhere around two o'clock in the afternoon, father would announce which relatives, grandparents, aunts, uncles, cousins, we were going to bless with our visit. If we didn't go to them, more than likely, some of them would drop by to see us. This was a customary happening in the world of my childhood. My parents were always happy to see extended family. Just before we would head out the door, father would lift his violin from its place on top of the piano. He seldom made social calls without it. This was particularly true when we visited his siblings. A visit to any one of them was sure to end in a jam session around the piano. In their growing up years, father's family formed a band. Each sibling relied on training their ears to search for notes and melodies on their instrument of choice. My grandfather played the bass drum. His steady rhythm was the glue that held the music together. More about the band later.

From the moment we set off on a journey, my father, the storyteller, would begin a captivating dissertation. Most often it would be about his childhood. When the words coming from his lips were, "I remember when....", we would look at each other, roll our eyes, and turn a far away gaze toward the landscape fading out of sight as the car cruised down the road. Then I thought father was just creating stories to entertain us which has merits of its own. Now I know his stories were not all conceived in his imagination even though he did have an innate way of looking at life through rose colored glasses. You could sometimes tell which were truths and which were fiction. When he escaped into truth his demeanor softened. His tall, conditioned shoulders, wilted under the weight of guarded pride as the rhythmic cadence of his voice began to turn the story into song. Father's eyes refused to hold his prosaic secrets. Squinting for detailed acuity, they illuminated his yarns allowing him to look into his time capsule at the 'crown jewels' of his life. Before long, laugh lines guarded the twinkle in his eyes and he was in the story.

On many a Sunday afternoon, soon after he turned the car north onto highway 281, he would begin. "Look, kids," he would say, just after he made the right turn onto highway 512 at Bouse Junction. We were on our way to see our grandparents. With deft skill he steered the car along the familiar road covered with rich red Oklahoma dirt. He slowed the car to glide down and over the hills. "This is Cheyenne Valley where I lived when I was a boy. See the mountains on each side of the road?" father continued. "I used to climb to the top of those peaks when I little. These are the Gloss Mountains. If you look close you can see sparkles of light in them. At times, the flickers look something like lightning bugs flitting about. Other times they are like tiny bits of glass glistening in the sunlight. That glint of light is made by the selenite in the mountain. Selenite is what covers the windows of the four burners of the cookstove in our kitchen. The sheer, fragile coverings on the windows of grandpa's old car were made of selenite. Before solid glass windows were invented, selenite was used to protect passengers from uncomfortable or inclimate weather. Another name for selenite is isenglass. I'm sure you remember the words of our state song Oklaho-ma..........with isenglass curtains that roll right down in case there's a change in the weather."

Father was telling a story. His story. He was reminiscing his past, bringing it into our present, and preserving it for our future. As his captive audience, we bounced along in our thirty-three ford with the holes in the floor and roof, pre-tending we were transfixed by the drama of his stories. With serene reverence, he continued his story.

# Chapter Twelve

O-SI-YO

Griever Canyon was the first scenic passageway we would drive through on our way to visit our grandparents. It was the straggling west end of the Gloss Mountain Range. At first sight, one might not think of this place as a canyon. Those who discover a distinct curve drop into a gulch framed by red rock channeling through the mountains might report otherwise. Roadside picnic tables nestled among the stately cedar make an ideal gathering place for an afternoon retreat. Next a lackadaisical cruise over the wooden bridge arching across the anonymous trickling stream near the bottom of the canyon. A quick push on the accelerator to gain momentum up the steep gradient exiting the canyon. Then we would continue on to Bouse Junction, a place where highways 412 and 281 inter-sected. Father turned right on 412 toward Cheyenne Valley in the gaping Gloss Mountain range.

The Gloss Mountains are a rare outcropping of buttes. For centuries, they have absorbed the historical transformation of events and people in northwestern Oklahoma. And still they stand staunch and sturdy and beautiful. It isn't any wonder my daddy loved their magnificent presence in the front door of his home in the valley of the Cheyenne. Griever Canyon was a part of this mountainous area. It was a playground for the community where

I grew up. When folks picnicked or celebrated special days, oft times they went to Griever Canyon. There were low red mountains to climb, streams complete with water and quicksand to wade, and dark mysterious canyons to explore which were once the hiding place of the Dalton Gang. Each year, on the last official day, our country school had a community wide picnic. Many of the town's folk turned out to celebrate whether they had children in school or not. There was lots of fried chicken, baloney sandwiches, potato salad, baked beans, pie, cake, and homemade ice cream.

One year, while folks were preparing the tables for lunch, six-year-old Dennis climbed up the face of the mountain near the picnic area. When he turned around to wave and cheer at those of us below a flood of fear surged through his small body and he froze to the side of the mountain. Tears of fright washed his ruddy cheeks and his lungs worked overtime. It was hard to fathom how he got up there much less how he was to be gotten down. With great haste, someone went back to town and returned with a strong and fearless young man who agreed to climb the mountain. Thus the rescue of Dennis. I rather doubt he has clambered up another mountain since.

"That mountain straight ahead is called Lone Mountain," father would begin. "One day my brothers and I scaled to the top of its highest peak to see if we could catch the eagle we believed was up there. We didn't catch the eagle but we discovered a tall earthen cone-like structure covered with the red clay of the mountains. Many years ago a band of Cheyenne Indians settled in the valley and built that cone. It was believed the Cheyennes used the mounds to send smoke signals to others in the Tribe. Sometimes the cone mounds were used in burial ceremonies. They used them as markers for other tribes following after them."

"When the Cheyennes and Cherokees were settled along the northern and southern boundaries of the Cimarron River many wild and wooly activities were still happening," Daddy continued. I am sure me and my brothers and sister probably rolled our eyes as a sign of disinterest. What aging has taught us is that Daddy was sharing the rich history of his youth. History that whether we liked it or not imprinted an indelible mark upon him and each one of us that would in some way make an infinite difference in our lives.

He kept the story going, "With spring rains that filled the rivers, there was lush grass for buffalo and cattle. This area where we are was considered open undivided lands where ranchers could drive their herds to market. In 1867, James G. McCoy established a cattle market in Abilene, Kansas. Most of the cattle in Texas were longhorns that sold for four dollars a head. Ranchers hoped they might go for forty in Abilene, Kansas. Close your eyes and imagine a thousand or more head of cattle with long sharp horns trumping along, being herded through here. The cows would probably stop to nibble on the grass. When they reached the river they might get a drink, and as the herd pushed against them they would test the depth of the water, reluctantly step into the river and swim to the other side. If ranchers had several thousand head of cattle it would cost them less to hire cowboys to drive them to market than to put them on some other kind of transportation." Daddy was always teaching common sense realities.

The Civil War had ended in 1865. Many from the Confederate cavalry, the freed ex-slaves, and Mexican gauchos were left without work. Now they seemed a ready work force of skilled horsemen for drovers. The year the war ended Jesse Chisholm established the Chisholm Trail that would become a major route for travel. It ran six hundred miles from San Antonio, Texas to Abilene, Kansas.

A drive of two thousand or more cattle required only a trail boss and a dozen cowhands. There were two big obstacles for cattle drives of this sort. First, the trail boss had to guide his mass of cattle along the eastern fringe of the Gloss Mountains where the Dalton Gang hid out. They were notorious criminals. Second, they had to cross rivers in Indian Territory and through meadows and terrains of lush grass and abundant American buffalo on Indian lands.

These were the water and food supply for the Indians. As one might imagine this made the Cheyenne less than happy. In an effort to protect the livelihood of the Tribe, they would attack the drovers and their cattle. Sometimes taking cattle, other times assaulting and killing cowhands. Consequently, the cowhands decided to take matters into their own hands. They intentionally and without justification killed the buffalo in an attempt to starve the Indians out of the Valley of the Cheyenne which had been designated a Reservation for the Cheyenne. Still the ranchers continued their cattle drives.

Can you just imagine seeing this astronomical mass of restless energy bumping, lumbering, sometimes out of control, two thousand times two huge horns buckling, grinding against one another and coming at you? Who would have ever thought that 'Once upon a time in Oklahoma there was a ragged version of the "Running of the Bulls (Longhorns, that is)" much like that in Pamplona, Spain? Lucky for us and the world, cattle drives of this nature ended in the late 1880's.

Even though the Cheyennes had moved on before my Webster family moved to the banks of the Cimarron, father reminisced in the drama of the stories told to him. He basked in the joy of his childhood memories. He took advantage of every possible opportunity to share his stories of life in the Valley of the Cheyenne. Riding along through the Valley on our way to visit grandparents, he would paint idyllic images of how life was when he was a child. When he talked about the red mountains that fortressed the Cimarron River on the south, his eyes would smile with a kind of euphoric pleasure. Father was a storyteller. What we thought were tales spun from his imagination were in fact, legends of truth cloaked in magic and mystery. He used the skillful techniques of a master story-teller.

# Chapter Thirteen

O-SI-YO

One of the most memorable stories daddy told was of an Indian Maiden believed to be of the Cherokee Tribe. His assertion was that she was our great grandmother.

As the story goes, she was a courageous young Cherokee maiden making her way through the Illinois mountains on a paint pony and with a papoose firmly strapped on her back. No one really knew who she was. No one knew who she was and why she carried an infant or what happened to her.

The consensus of my Webster family was that the infant was a part of our ancestry. Thus, the DNA of the family was changed. With that analogy, the family has lived in the mysterious euphoria of the story. It is a puzzlement that binds all family ties. It inspires all kinds of questions. Such as who was this mysterious woman? Who were the parents of the child? Where was the Indian Maiden going?

This became an "X" factor in the family. My quest has been to identify or justify the specific relationship suggested here or to just embrace the possible ramifications of the mystique.

# Chapter Fourteen

## O-SI-YO

  Heat penetrated the humid air when daddy stopped the car in front of the old abandoned bank building in Seiling, Oklahoma. A few years earlier the bank had moved to a new building across the street. Even though the ground floor of the old bank was no longer occupied, the Masonic Order continued to hold its bi-monthly meetings on the second level.

  It was like an explosion. The doors of the car flew open and with haste, all four of us kids jumped out. This was one of the few times our parents allowed us to exercise our growing independence. While they were socializing with the Order of Eastern Stars we were granted the privilege of going to the movies.

  "Here is a dime for your ticket and a nickel for a bag of popcorn," father said. "Remember to sit together, be quiet and don't bother other people. We'll come get you when the meeting is over." Then he turned to my older brother and sister and said, "Marion, you and Joan look after the twins. (that meant Donald and me)." With our dime and nickel white-knuckled in our hot little hands, we took our leave and rounded the corner toward the theater. As quick as a bolt of lightning, our steps came to a near halt. In the darkness of the recessed doorway of the old bank, a man, perhaps an old man, sat in silence. It was too dark to tell anything about his age. He was positioned on the stoop with his legs bent underneath as a cushion for his body and appeared to be wrapped in some kind of heavy blanket. It was August in Oklahoma and the very hot temperatures didn't require a blanket. Quite possibly we might have thought "to each his own" and continued on our way. "Come on. Let's hurry. It is almost time for the movie to start," Marion whispered. As we scurried along, thoughts of the mysterious man in the shadows were soon forgotten.

Midway down the street we could see the bright lights surrounding the glass window of the box office where Mrs. Cates, the owner of the theater, sold the tickets. Others hoping to see the movie had formed a line on the sidewalk in front of the theater. We slowed our steps, mustered our dignity and fell in line behind the others. As was usual, when it came our turn to buy a ticket, Mrs. Cates gave each of us a stern look over her eyeglasses and asked, "How old are you?" Below 10 years old, paid 10 cents for a ticket. The cost for those above was 25 cents. Once she was assured we were in the younger age bracket, we forfeited our dimes and she handed us the coveted ticket.

The dazzling lights above the box office accentuated the marquee broadcasting the title of the movie being shown. They blinked in synchronized rhythm luring us into the hex of another episode of Ma and Pa Kettle Back On The Farm. It was a part of a series of two others we'd seen with the same theme and identical character actors. This third segment was a slap-stick situation comedy depicting an earthy couple's visit to New York City. I guess the kindest thing to say about the character of Pa in these drama was that he was a dreamer. His slight build exuded fragility when, in fact, he was a man of generous determination. Pa went about the farm with his head erect, eyes twirled toward the clouds, and with detached, poker-faced expressions. All giving air to a man in search of perceptions beyond the ordinary. He was always coming up with grandiose schemes to impress Ma.

On the other hand, Ma was full figured, stocky and robust. She twisted her brownish locks into a loose bun that bobbed about on top of her head. Then placing her hands on her more than ample waist, she declared Pa's tactics quick-witted and clever. Ma spoke with authority. Her character was delightfully innocent and hopeful. She could be swayed to participate in Pa's outlandish ideas. The pivotal point of this movie came in the scene where Ma and Pa were walking down Fifth Avenue in New York City. All of a sudden Pa had one of his ingenious revelations. The cultural glamour of city life had gotten to him, inspiring his explorer instincts. He decided they should return to the farm and look for uranium. Uranium? On the farm? Does that make sense? Well, no, but that is how things work in the movies.

As we entered the theater we could hear the pop, pop, popping of corn in the glassed in machine. The golden kernels seemed to be in competition to be the one that could leap the highest to the rhythmic sounds as they burst into large white puffs. When the metal cooking bowl filled to the brim the fresh popcorn cascaded over the sides like rapids of snow. We were enthralled by the heavy fragrance of the hot corn laced with butter. With haste, each of us handed our nickel to Mrs. Cates. She lifted the bags from under the warming lights of the machine and we made haste to find our seat in the theater.

The theater floor sloped downward toward the viewing screen. We chose to sit half way to the front. Soon after settling in our seats, Tom and Jerry cartoons appeared on the screen. We were mesmerized at the antics of Tom, the rascally Cat, and Jerry, the daring mouse all the while nibbling on soporific popcorn. After the cartoons, a news reel highlighting events happening around the world was shown. For me, the most impressionable clips portrayed developments in World War II which was happening as we were being entertained. Next were previews of upcoming movies. This was our way of knowing what movies we could anticipate in the future. Newspapers announcing upcoming entertainment events and distributed in rural towns were published in metropolitan areas and were particular to those areas.

Soon after the previews, the theater lights went up and Mrs. Cates parted the heavy curtains separating the lobby (I use the term lobby loosely as it was a space limited to not more than six people.) from the auditorium. With stalwart preci-sion, she made her way down the center aisle, never stopping until she was standing directly in front of the large black screen. In her arms, she carried a heavy jar with tiny papers inside. On the back of each, was a seat number.

A hush settled over the room. One night each week, Mrs. Cates had a drawing. The prize was a free movie pass for the person sitting in the seat with a number matching the one drawn from the jar. She asked Wylie Littleman, a Native American classmate of ours, to help her determine the winner. He slid his hand in the jar and pulled out a slip of paper. Mrs. Cates called out, "number twenty-nine." In delightful anticipation, everyone looked at the back of their seat to confirm the number. Our brother Marion was sitting in seat number twenty-nine. All of us were excited when Marion's number was drawn. That meant sometime soon we could return to see another movie. Our parents would not want him to go to the movies alone so we'd have to make the sacrifice to go with him. The MGM lion roared on the screen and the movie began.

As promised, when the movie was over our parents were waiting outside the theater. On our way to the car, we made a wide detour around the dark entrance where we had seen the figure in the shadows. We peeked in his direction. He continued to sit in silence. After we got in the car, we told mother and father about Marion winning the free movie pass and about the person sitting in the dark entrance niche of the old bank. They made a possible assumption that the man might be someone of the Cheyenne/Arapaho native American Tribe.

Mother said, "Sometimes, even on days when it is very hot, they wrap themselves in a tribal blanket and seek solitude in unsuspecting places." This was probably one of the first times I was made aware of the presence of native Americans living in the community. Yes, Wylie Littleman was of Cheyenne/Arapaho descent, but he was a friend. We never thought in terms of his ethnicity. Even though father had told us stories about remnants of the Cherokee and Cheyenne/Arapaho Tribes having lived near his boyhood home in northwest Oklahoma, we didn't connect the dots that put all of it together.

# Chapter Fifteen

## O-SI-YO

    I want to tell you the story of one of the three most courageous spirits I know of in my Webster family. Sarah Jane Webster's life was fraught with tumultuous events from the earliest beginnings of her life. One of the reasons I want you to know her story is because she was my paternal great grandmother. the mother of my grandmother Sarah Melinda Smith Webster. In many ways, Sarah Jane was a victim of the times.

    Her father Francis Marion Webster I was my paternal second great grandfather. He was married to Lucinda Kennedy. They had three children. Sarah Jane Webster (1847), was their first born. Her sister, Mary Ann Webster was born in 1849, and a brother, William Webster was born in 1850. Sarah Jane's mother Lucinda Kennedy Webster died in 1850 probably as a result of William's birth. She was nineteen years old. At the time, Sarah Jane was three years old.

    Soon after Lucinda's death, as in almost immediately following her demise, Sarah Jane's father, Francis Marion Webster I took a second wife, Hester Widger. Hester became the stepmother of Sarah Jane and her two siblings. Then, as one would expect, Francis Marion I and Hester added five more children to the family dynamics. In 1859, Sarah Jane's father Francis Marion Webster I died. Now Hester was left to parent eight children all under twelve years of age. Twelve year old Sarah Jane was orphaned along with her younger sister and brother. I can only imagine how stressful this circumstance might be for a stepmother or any mother, as far as that goes to parent eight children in the mid 1800's.

I don't know the details but whatever they were, sometime between 1860-1869, teenager Sarah Jane met a young man named Elisha Smith. Not much is known about Elisha. What is known is that Sarah Jane and Elisha shared the same birth year, 1847. They were fourteen years old.

In 1861, these two fourteen year olds married. Probably not an uncommon happening in the 1800's. In 1863, these then sixteen year olds, had a daughter named Sarah Melinda Smith. Then to keep a roof over their heads, Sarah Jane hired out as a live-in housekeeper for a Dr. Elias Mimson from Ohio. (Dr. Mimson, a widower, was the local doctor and real estate representative.) There is evidence that Sarah Jane continued to live and work with Dr. Mimson after she gave birth to Sarah Melinda.

There is no documentation regarding Elisha Smith's whereabouts until in 1865 when he joined the Union Army. He was in the Cavalry of Regiment 61. In 1869, he was listed as a casualty of the Civil War. Elisha's death appears espe-cially tragic. One report indicated that he sold his horse along with it's raiments, his canteen, and his firearm, complete with ammunition, to the enemy. For that, he was brought before a military trial, was charged with treason, pronounced guilty, and was executed on the spot. I take personal consolation in not being able to authenticate this story. But can one just imagine such a horrific scenario?

A few years after Elisha's death, Sarah Jane married George Washington McCaslin. Aunt Jennie Chaffee (my father's sister) reported that George W. McCaslin was not a kind stepfather. More to the point, he was a mean spirited person, jealous, short fused temperament, and restrictive. He didn't believe Sarah Jane's daughter Sarah Melinda should go to school. Instead, he lashed out threats of intimidation to oppress her desire to learn. Today, we might call him a male chauvinist who saw females as stay at home workhorses, learn to cook, plow the fields, become a seamstress, and make garments for others as a source of household income.

His punitive behavior toward Sarah Jane's daughter, led Sarah Jane to look for a way to insure her child a safer and more compassionate home life.

With both of Sarah Jane's parents deceased, direct family support was not available. It is suspected that it was difficult for her to care for Sarah Melinda and fulfill her duties for the good doctor. Sidney Ellen Widger Webster and George Washington Webster II (Sarah Melinda's great aunt and uncle) took Sarah Melinda into their home to stay on a limited basis. I suppose in today's world we know this as babysitting.

Sidney Ellen Widger Webster would return her to her mother from time to time. This arrangement continued through out Sarah Melinda's young childhood. When she was about thirteen years old she made the choice to live with Sidney Ellen Widger Webster and George Washington Webster II. They had five children. Sarah Melinda was especially fond of George Washington Webster II's son Francis Marion Webster, who had changed his name to Marion Francis Webster I. When the two came of age they married. They were my paternal grandparents.

I tell you Sarah Jane's story because it reminds me of the steady determination of the spirit of those who went before us. The losses and hardships they endured. A human spirit full of tenacity and compassion.

Sarah Jane had one sister and one brother. She died in 1917 at the age of 70.

# Chapter Sixteen

O-SI-YO

The Webster family originated in England, probably somewhere in the vicinity of London. It is quite possible that in the late afternoon of September, 1750, a Kings Passenger Ship from London carrying rapturous human cargo of highly charged immigrants docked along the shores of Virginia. It is also plausible that my fourth great grandfather, Richard John Webster, might have been on board with those expectant travelers. He brought with him his wife Rebecca Robertson Webster and a young son John Richard Webster who became my third great grandfather.

I can't fathom how they must have felt when they set foot on the soil of this foreign place. Nor can I grasp the reality of integrating with the original inhabitants, the Native American Indians, who had arrived many years before them and who may not have been exactly thrilled to have total strangers encroach on their territory. With courage and grit, they settled into the rigorous colonial lifestyle of Virginia.

In the late 1700"s, John Richard Webster and his wife, Margaret, migrated to Tennessee where they had a family of several children. Their son, born in 1790, named George Washington Webster I, married Elizabeth (Betsy) Hubbard in 1819. Together they gave birth to five children, three singles and one set of fraternal twins, Narcissa and Francis Marion Webster who became Sarah Jane Webster's father as noted above.

Just a little sideline to those in the Webster lineage who are interested in the twin gene factor.... Well, I can assure you there is one. There are fraternal twins as well as identical ones. In families many times the question is asked regarding multiple births. No one I knew in the Webster family could answer that question. As it turns out research reveals twins in several generations. In 1826, fraternal twins Francis Marion Webster and Narcissi Webster Coyle were born to George Washington Webster I and Elizabeth Hubbard. Born in 1855 to Francis Marion Webster and his then wife Lucinda Kennedy was a set of twin boys, James T. and John E. Webster. Twin daughters, Emaline and Angeline (1843) were born to Levi Webster and Nancy Kennedy. Another set of twin girls, Hannah and Ra-chel was born to Andrew Webster and Elizabeth Austin in 1871. Fraternal twins Donna and Donald were born in 1936 to Dewey and Irene Webster.

After gold was discovered on reservations belonging to the Indians, the United States Government began it's quest to persuade the Indians to forfeit their land for what was supposedly a healthy five million dollars. Plus a permanent, possibly grandiose home in Indian Territory, Oklahoma was thrown into the pot of seduction. To some, this was thought a good deal. To others, it smelled of the trickery of a pythoness. Strife, unrest, and division grew between the Indians and the government that promised a deal they would soon learn was 'too good to be true.' To date, the five million has never been paid to the Indians and to lay claim on this idyllic Indian Territory many would lose their lives. And where was this place called Indian Territory, Oklahoma? President Andrew Jackson became impatient with the Indians and imposed the Removal Act of the Native American Indian Tribes from the eastern sector of the United States to the assigned Indian Territory in Oklahoma. Because so many lives were lost, some 4,000 in this cruel expulsion of these trusting and unsuspecting people, history records this as the Trail of Tears (1838-1839).

At the time, Cheyenne/Arapaho and Cherokee Tribes remained in Major and Woods Counties of northern Oklahoma.

Then in 1912, after the Indians moved on west, Marion Francis Webster I, my grandfather, patented a tract of land along the southern banks of the Cimarron River in Woods County, Oklahoma aka Indian Territory. Soon after, his son-in-law, Kay Gould, ran into financial difficulties on a tract of land he had acquired through one of the seven official Land Runs. Grandfather assumed his loan at the bank and took ownership. Over a short period of time, grandfather picked up a grand total of 478.38 acres all skirting the banks of the restless Cimarron River. This became the Webster Ranch where my father, Dewey S. Webster lived out his youth.

The Webster clan began the long journey from Tennessee to Indian Territory, Oklahoma sometime around 1825. Three generations of this group settled in the area around Chicago, Illinois. This is where my grandfather Marion Francis Webster I was born. Their trek to Illinois included the families of George Washington Webster I (1790) and wife Elizabeth (Betsy) Hubbard.

George Washington Webster II (1829-1906) and their son Marion Francis I (1861-1930) and Sarah Melinda Smith (1863-1934) all lived in Illinois. While in Illinois Marion Francis and Sarah Melinda had four children. Then, in October of 1887, the Websters left Illinois in a covered wagon because they believed job opportunities were better further west, they pushed on to Eureka, Kansas. Prior to moving to Greenwood County, Kansas, Marion Francis Webster I worked on the railroad. During their time in Kansas, they had seven additional children one of whom was my father Dewey S. Webster.

Some took advantage of the Land Runs to obtain land on which to live. Others participated in allotment or sealed bids for a parcel of land to call their own. Those filing for land grants were expected to make improvements on the property within seven years or to buy it outright at market value. Not complying with this requirement, forced them to forfeit their chosen parcel of land.

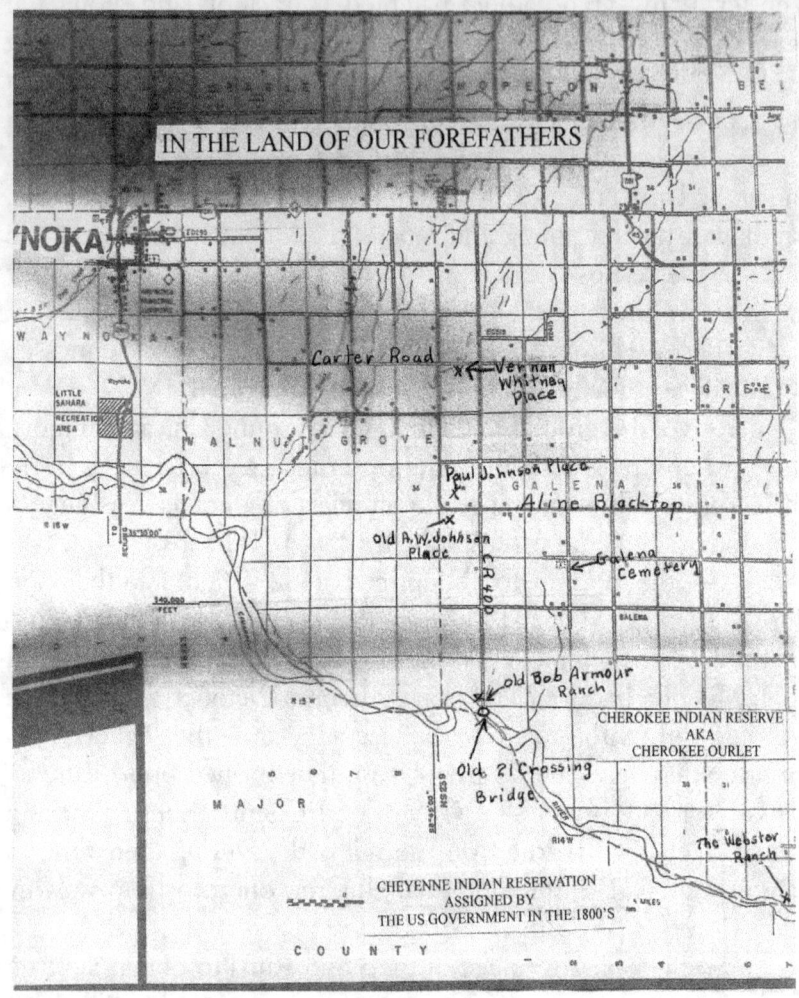

IN THE MID 1800'S, THE US GOVERNMENT SENT THE CHEYENNE INDIAN TRIBE TO INDIAN TERRITORY, OKLAHOMA TO LIVE. A RESERVATION WAS CREATED FOR THEM ON THE SOUTH SIDE OF THE CIMARRON RIVER IN INDIAN TERRITORY, OKLAHOMA. THE TRIBE WAS HAPPY.

A FEW YEARS LATER AND FOLLOWING THE TRAIL OF TEARS FIASCO, A SMALL SECTOR OF THE CHEROKEE INDIAN TRIBE ARRIVED WITH PLANS TO LAY CLAIM ON THE SAME AREA. UNDER THE TREATIES OF 1828 AND 1835 AND AFTER CONFLICT AND ANGUISH OVER SHARING THEIR NEW HOMELAND WITH THE CHEYENNES, THE US GOVERNMENT STEPPED IN. SEVEN MILLION ACRES OF LAND WAS GIVEN TO THE CHEROKEE NATION ALONG WITH A PARCEL OF LAND 58 MILES WIDE AND 220 MILES LONG ACROSS THE NORTHERN BORDER OF THE STATE AS A TRIBAL HUNTING GROUND, KNOWN AS THE CHEROKEE OUTLET. THIS TOOK IN THE AREA ON THE NORTH SIDE OF THE CIMARRON RIVER. NOW BOTH TRIBES HAD ACCESS TO THE SUPPLY OF BUFFALO, LUSH GRASSLANDS, AND WATER FROM THE RIVER.

# Chapter Seventeen

## O-SI-yo

Marion Francis Webster I, my grandfather, left his family in Kansas and worked odd jobs to defray costs for his journey into Indian Territory, Oklahoma and to place a sealed bid on a piece land for a home to accommodate his family.

Grandfather had worked at the Woodrow Ranch in Kansas. Then again, when he was in route to his destination in Oklahoma, he worked on another ranch. All the while he was saving money to afford to place a sealed bid on land along the Cimarron River in Indian Territory.

The 101 Ranch south of Ponca City, Oklahoma was owned by Colonel George Washington Miller, a veteran of the Confederate Army in 1893. Before statehood was established Miller migrated from Kentucky after the Civil War. For a while, he settled in Missouri, then he drove cattle from Texas to railway heads in Kansas. Quite possibly fording the Cimarron River in Woods and Major Counties where my grandparents acquired lands under sealed bids. After the Colonel died in 1903, his sons Joe, George, and Zack continued operating the 101 ranch. The ranch was some 110,000 acres on the northern prairie of Indian Territory. The Colonel's vision was that the Ranch be as self sustaining and diversified as possible. Livestock of all kinds cattle, bison, hogs (more than 10,000 hogs were shipped to market per year), poultry and several breeds of horses. Wheat, cotton, corn, alfalfa, fruit orchards, and a variety of vegetables were produced. There was a meat processing plant, a post office, a grocery store, an electric plant, a cannery. a dairy, a tannery, and several different mills. The Ranch was a not so miniature town.

As impressive as the Ranch was, it got its notoriety from the Wild West Show starring Buffalo Bill. It was an entertainment extravaganza mixing rodeo an circus acts. The Wild West Show travelled all around, even went to Europe.

It is not difficult to imagine that with the magnitude of the operations of the Ranch and the spectacular Wild West Show, walk in cowboys, ranch hands. clowns. and conductors of magic could be assured a job. Grandfather Marion Francis Webster I was, for a moment in history, a Foreman on the most notorious Ranch ever known. Even so, he was a man on a mission to claim his own piece of red earth.

In a short time, Grandfather Marion Francis Webster I placed a sealed bid on property offered by the government. In part, it was land once designated as a Cheyenne Indian Reservation. Even though the Cheyennes had disseminated in the late 1800's, their spirits hung around to join the hearts of those who would carry them into the future. Grandfather's bid proposal was accepted and he became the proud owner of a piece of land richly laden with mystical images and customs of God's sacred earth in Indian Territory. To be good stewards of this precious parcel of land, was a perfect fit for the Websters. They were known as "tillers of the soil."

After securing a piece of land, Grandfather sent for his family. Sarah Melinda loaded the children and all their belongings into their covered wagon and headed toward Indian Territory, in the valley of the Cheyennes. They experienced the rough western lifestyle when they settled on their remote ranch in Major County Oklahoma along the Cimarron River.

On the ranch, the Webster's held Sunday afternoon rodeos in the open field on their property and a cloud of dust hovered over the long trail leading toward the Webster Ranch along the Cimarron

River as the cloth covered roadsters made their approach. They created a knock off version of a wild west show that mimicked the one on the 101 Ranch in Ponca City. It was complete with a musical band (family band) in a bandstand, an arena formed by cars of those who came to participate and witness the rodeo, and clowns to provide a buffer for the bull ride events. They parked their cars in a large semi-circle forming a place for the calf roping, bucking broncs, barrel riding, and bull riding, etc.

The Webster Family Band gathered on the bandstand near one side of the arena. Upon the downbeat of their music, the rodeo parade made its entrance. My father was the first to enter the arena. He rode a sleek black stallion and carried a large American flag bearing the red, white, and blue stripes. Other riders who were participating in the rodeo followed him. Of course the clowns joined in the show. They were rolling large barrels around in an attempt to entertain and to assure the crowd they were ready to assist should a cowboy be in danger of an animal gone wild and dispirited during the show.

After the parade dismissed, the rodeo announcer would call the first event. Most of the time. it was the cowboys riding bucking broncos, then the calf roping, next the women's barrel races, the bull riding and team-tying. Each participant was timed to determine the level of his/her success. All made for an exciting afternoon.

Webster Family Band

# Chapter Eighteen

*0-SI-yo*

Father basked in the joy of his childhood memories. He took advantage of every possible opportunity to share his stories of life in the Valley of the Cheyenne. Riding along through the Valley on our way to visit grandparents, he would paint idyllic images of how life was when he was a child When he talked about the red mountains that fortressed the Cimarron River on the south, his eyes would smile with a kind of euphoric pleasure. Father was a storyteller. What we thought were tales spun from his imagination were in fact legends of truth cloaked in magic and mystery. He used the skillful techniques of a master story-teller.

Life on the Webster Ranch meant they didn't see anybody outside their family for two weeks or more. And it meant milking thirty head of cows each day and building fences to keep the cattle in the pastures. Church was a six mile ride in the horse drawn buggy.

The Webster's were hard working people and they were fun loving people who knew how to entertain themselves. Grandfather's inspiration and tutelage fostered in each child a love of music. He nurtured their skills to play musical in-struments. The Webster children were strong willed. This unique family birthed a musical band that played for parties, weddings. dances, rodeos, and many other events.  According to my father's sister, Aunt Jenny Chaffee, my father, Dewey Webster, was the one in the family with the most innate musical talent.  He had a good sense of rhythm, a keen ear for differentiating sounds, and could play most any instrument—the piano, the trumpet. the trombone, the guitar, and the violin.  Years later he taught my brother Marion Francis to play the piano.

  Every Sunday the Websters held a concert in the living room of their home.  They invited anyone who enjoyed music to come  They loved to entertain.  Sarah Melinda, their mother, did not play in the band.  It was said she had a beautiful singing voice.  Every summer's day, Sarah Melinda tucked a flower from her garden behind the tight stylish bun on the back of her head.  When the band played out in the yard, she sat on a milk bucket in the shade of the sycamore tree and kept time with the music.

  Since the Webster's lived on a farm, far out in the country, they could practice their music in the yard without bothering the neighbors.  However, it is reported that friends on neighboring farms would schedule the completion of their chores around the Webster's evening practice.  Then they would bring chairs from their houses to their yards to sit and listen to the music.  Colonel, the Webster family dog, was not too thrilled about the music.  He howled and whined until the last note echoed away.  I wonder if he was named after Colonel Miller who owned the 101 Ranch near Ponca City.

  Grandfather fashioned a special wagon with jet bunting attached around the outside bottom edge of the bed.  This was used to carry the band members and their instruments when they played for events away from home.  The wagon was pulled by two identical gray horses adorned with sparkling silver halters.  The red, white, and blue bunting swayed in rhythm to the prancing of the horses as they made their way down the crusty red clay country roads.  Oh, it was a smart sight to behold.

Dewey Sampson Webster

Marion Francis Webster I

The Hess Ranch was near the Webster family home. Each summer the Hess family hosted a rodeo. One year the Hess rodeo featured a horse race for women only. Mr. Hess wagered a bet on a horse race between his wife Flora Bell and my aunt Marguerite Webster. The Websters were horse people. The had more than an ample stable of horses from which to choose. Marguerite's favorite was Sunny, a sleek auburn filly Grandpa Webster had given her three years ago when the foal was born. But for this race she decided to ride Grandpa's horse, Red Wing, a beautiful reddish brown sorrel. Red Wing was a spirited stallion always chomping at the bit ready for excitement. Flora Bell was riding Sun Devil, a solid black horse known for his speed and agility. One regulation to qualify for the race was that the riders had to be able to put their feet in the stirrups. That was not a problem for Flora Bell who was taller and of a more mature stature than Marguerite. Marguerite, a teenager, was short and stalky. She had always ridden bareback and didn't know if her feet would fit in the stirrups. The night before the race she went to the barn to make sure she could reach the stirrups. It was a snug stretch. She would have to work hard to keep her feet through the stirrups.

Another ranch bordering next to the Webster ranch belonged to the Jess Howard family. The Howards were a black family, the only black family for many miles around. We were always taught a great deal of respect for them. Just think on this scenario. It was 1912 in Indian Territory. They were the only black family out in backwoods country of this newly inaugurated State and surrounded by white families. They were so brave and trusting. Father told stories of the interactions of the two families. The Howards were a kind and neighborly family. Jess was a man who loved riding the bucking horses, even rode the hot, angry, snorting bulls, and team calf roped with other ranchers on Sunday afternoons at the Webster rodeos. My favorite story about Jess and his wife, Mary, is about the day after my twin and I was born. They came, as did so many others, to see "the twins." But Jess and Mary were tentative in their approach to our bassinets. They explained to our mother that they were afraid since they were black they might frighten us. My throat tightens when I think of this special family

# Rodeo Arena
## Webster and Hess Ranches

who are now among the spirits that linger in my soul.

Now Marguerite was making ready for the women's horse race at the rodeo. Her mother Sarah Melinda Webster made her a special outfit to wear for the race. Dark brown trousers with gold fringe down the sides and a red silk shirt. Perched on top of her long black hair was brother Delbert's cowboy hat. She looked the part of a serious horse woman.

Early in the morning the day of the race, skies were overcast. By two o'clock in the afternoon, dark clouds began to gather in the west. The Rodeo announcer called contestants in the Women's race to the Starting Line. With confidence, Flora Bell coaxed Sun Devil toward the line. Marguerite Webster held a tight rein on Red Wing. He turned his head this way and that. His eyes like head lamps piercing the distance. Marguerite tightened his rein. He was poised on the starting line ready for the gun shot to be fired giving permission to leap to the Finish.

In that instance, a crack of lightning split the sky, followed by a thunderous boom from the heavens, a wall of rain pummeled the crowd and everyone ran into the woods for cover. Race ended.

Another time, Aunt Jenny Webster, Marguerite's sister, wanted to ride Molly the big grey horse Marguerite always rode. With the slightest provocation, that horse could be too spooky for an inexperienced rider. The older siblings were told to watch out for Jenny and above all, not let her get on Marguerite's horse. Jenny wanted to ride like all the other kids.

One day when their parents were away, Jenny begged and pleaded with the others to let her get on Molly. With a word of warning, Marguerite helped her climb onto Molly's back. Then she cautioned Jenny again, "Just sit on Molly's back. That is all. Don't do anything else. Above all, do not tell her to go or kick her sides." Jenny sat very still for a mo-ment. Her feet dangled against Molly's sides. Then she clicked her tongue as she had heard her older siblings do.

Molly knew that sound. She took a step, then another, followed by another, and another. Then she took off running, revving up at break neck speed. Jenny had a death grip on Molly's reins. "Help," she screamed. Molly was searching for a way back to the barn lot.  Now she was on a dead run.  Nothing could stop her.  Still Jenny hung onto her back.  She was going so fast she could not stop when she saw the gate to the lot.  Molly slid to a sudden stop, her front hooves plowed under the gate, horse and rider rested on the ground.  Later when Jenny was telling this story she explained, "I don't know what made me do it.  Maybe the devil got into me."

I think it is fair to say the Webster children were strong willed and adventuresome.  They were magnificent conglomerates of those two amoebae, of the Websters and the Smiths, in our ancestral swim.  Some of my fondest memories are of times the Webster siblings would gather as a family.  They remembered their parents, told stories of their childhood, played their instruments, sang in harmony, and danced until they had expended every drop of energy within themselves.

Thanksgiving was the day they chose to celebrate together.  Every year they gathered early in the day at the home of one sibling or the other.  The men garbed in rugged clothes, with rifles or shotguns slung over their shoulders ready to stalk the pastures and fields in search of quail or pheasant.  My uncle, Marion Francis Webster the Second, my father's brother, was a reputable dentist from Dallas, Texas.  He would bring along his dog Lucky to assist in spotting the birds and retrieving them once they were on the ground.  (My father always went along for the camaraderie but he never killed a bird. He never owned a gun or a firearm of any kind.  Father had a tender heart.)

Along about eleven o'clock in the morning the hunt would end and the men would return to the house with their offerings for the festive meal.  The ladies would pitch in, clean the birds, and fry them in a hot skillet glazed with lard.  Then the feast was complete.  A blessing was offered.  And such eating and rejoicing is hard to imagine.

When everyone had their fill one by one the siblings brought out their instruments.  My father got out his violin, someone went to their car to retrieve their trumpet, another a trombone, my mother or Marion, my older brother, usually filled in at the piano.  One year they played with such fervor as others danced with unbridled euphoric ecstasy, I feared our little four room frame house would implode and come crashing down around us. I remember sitting on the floor in the corner of our small living room tapping my foot with guarded zest to the rhythm of the music.

In time, the grandchildren of George Washington Webster II and Sidney Ellen Widger who were also the sons and daughters of Marion Francis Webster I and Sarah Melinda Smith Webster, left the family ranch. They chose to established themselves in various places from Oklahoma to Kansas to Montana.

I suppose every family believes theirs is a unique tribe of sojourners and indeed they are. Each has its own distinctive characteristics. The Webster family is composed of a duplicity of DNA genes. English, Welsh, Native American. Maybe that is what decrees some of us prim and proper like the English, some shy and strong as the Welsh, and others gentle, quiet, striving to live in harmony with the earth like our Native American brothers. Most of us are quite possibly more like melting pots of all the Webster ethnicity. I think we are who we are and that is the real blessing in this scenario.

I like to believe our family came forth from unleavened loaves bearing hope and joy. Reality reflects that we came into a leavened world filled with the enticements of the aromatic yeasts that threatened to lure us into the malignancy of darkness. We live in gratitude for the redemption offered through our faith in God's promise to be with us always. In His light, we continue to live every day with aspirations toward the fulfillment of our beautiful dreams.

As we trace the composite of those who gather around our table to break bread, it is more than appropriate or proper that we bow and give thanks for those on whose shoulders we stand, to render blessings upon those with us now, and to pray direction for those who will follow in our footsteps.

See page 113 for a map of Webster Ranch.

# Chapter Nineteen

O-SI-YO

The Cimarron River played an important part of our lives. It flowed between the farms of both our maternal and paternal grandparents. For the most part the river flowed gracefully along. The portion of the Cimarron River significant to this story runs between highway 281 on the west and Orienta, Oklahoma on the east. The river flows at an angle from far northwest Oklahoma east to near Tulsa, Oklahoma where it joins the Arkansas River. In the past, it played a prominent role in the development of the west.

Prior to statehood the Cherokee Indian Tribe occupied much of the land in the eastern part of the state. A small number of Cherokees followed the river westward and set up camp on the north side of the Cimarron. Earlier the Chey-enne had claimed the south side. The marauding Cheyenne, Comanche, Kiowa, Arapaho, and Apache Tribes roamed through and encamped in the northern part of the state. Large herds of buffalo roamed the prairies providing good food supply for the Indians. After the Five Civilized Tribes were moved to the western territory of the state, the warring tribes continued using the land. The civilized tribes didn't care much for their warring counterparts occupying their land and taking their food supply. So there were uprisings.

In 1867, following the Civil War of 1860-1865, the

government interceded with the disgruntled Indians. The land on the north of the Cimarron was given to the Cherokees and became known as part of the Cherokee Outlet. A reservation for the Cheyenne and Arapaho Tribes was created on the south. This seemed a good arrangement, as the Cimarron was a never-ending source of water for the Indians as well as a natural boundary identifying the specific territories the Tribes were to occupy. But it was an obstruction for cattlemen trying to get their cattle to market. Cattle had to ford the river, and to do so, they had to be driven through lands belonging to the Indians.

In this time, cattle markets were opening up in Kansas City. Cattlemen drove their herds to market via two major trails, the Great Western and the Chisholm Trails. One of these trails led north through Alva, Oklahoma toward Dodge City, Kansas. The other wound its way north through Kiowa, Kansas ending at the railhead in Abilene, Kansas. These trails were good for the ranchers as they went across open country where there was an abundance of free grazing. But the free grazing was through Indian Territory.

With the supply of buffalo becoming increasingly limited, the Indians grew restless and impatient with the white man and his cattle invading the territory and consuming the grass. They began committing terrible atrocities against the white man in an effort to remove him completely from their land. All this dissension opened the door for criminal ac-tivity. Thus, in 1891, the Dalton Gang terrorized this part of Indian Territory. Bob Dalton was the infamous leader of the group. In later years, William Dalton, brother of Bob, used the caves and canyons in the Gloss Mountains to hide from the authorities. For a time, he may have even holed up in Griever Canyon ten miles north of Seiling, Oklahoma. For eighteen months, the band of Dalton thugs kept both the red man and the white man on edge.

Before statehood there were few places Indians, cattlemen or gangs could cross the Cimarron. Dave Griever and a man named Houghton owned what was known as the "21" Ranch. The northern border of the ranch was about two and one half miles north of the Cimarron River and extended twenty miles south of the river. In the midst of the ranch stood the majestic Gloss

Mountains, Cheyenne Valley, Griever Canyon, and the Cimarron River.

Most of the time the Cimarron ambled along in slow motion allowing horse and buggy to cross, but when spring rains provoked its anger there was violence in its waters like none ever known. At times like those, crossing the Cimarron was treacherous at best. Before access was created, most folks prayed for low water levels and forded the river to get to the other side. It was common knowledge that when you started across the Cimarron you needed to plan on going the entire breadth of the river. There was no turning back. And stopping in the middle of the river was at risk of getting caught in quicksand with little hope of continuing on your journey.

Sometime between 1903-1909, a one half mile bridge was constructed across the Cimarron to provide access to towns and areas north of the river. And since it was located within the "21" Ranch owned by Griever and Houghton, it became known as the "21" Crossing to cattlemen who drove their herds up from Texas to markets in Abilene and Kansas City, Kansas. The "21" Crossing was constructed out of wooden planks with short single wooden plank railings lining each side to prevent those crossing from falling overboard. This is the bridge I knew as a child. And this is the bridge that left a memorable impression on my life.

# Chapter Twenty

## O-SI-YO

In the early 1900's, two families settled along the Cimarron River, near the "21" Ranch. The Webster Ranch was on the north side of the river with some land lying immediately across the river to the south. The Johnson family farm was about six miles north and west of the Webster Ranch. These two families held the keys to the biological origin of who I was to become.

In 1906, Marion F. Webster I moved his family from Kenner, Kansas in Greenwood County, Kansas to Major County, Oklahoma. The Webster Ranch, most likely a part of the original "21" Ranch, was located north of the Golden Valley School in Cheyenne Valley and geographically on the south side of the Cimarron River. This was home to my father, Dewey Webster, and his eleven siblings. The Webster family loved the land. They were proud to be ranchers. But more than anything, they were risk takers who enjoyed creating something new and exciting. They had an undeniable zest for life.

Living along the Cimarron could have been lonely except for the Webster spirit. To amuse themselves they formed a musical band. Each member of the family with the exception of Sarah Webster, my grandmother, played an instrument. She didn't play in the band but she encouraged everyone else. My father was the floating musician, so to speak. He could play any instrument that was needed. Grandfather Webster, (Marion Francis), played the bass drum. He set the rhythm for the family band.

The Webster Band played for all kinds of celebrations around the community—weddings, anniversaries, funerals, and rodeos. On hot summer evenings, they would take their instruments outside and practice. The neighbors tried to finish their daily chores in time to sit outside and listen to the Webster Band fine tune their music. None of the Webster children had music lessons. They learned to play by listening closely to the changing sounds within the music. It was called playing by ear. Daddy always had this heaven-sent smile on his face when he was wrapped up in playing his violin or whatever instrument.

Even after they had all left the family nest, when someone called a family gathering, they brought their instruments. After eating, they brought out their instruments and struck up a tune, several tunes. Some would play a while, then stop to dance a while. It was like watching children bask in the thrill of be-ing with old friends again. Any opportunity to sharpen their auditory skills in harmonizing with one another touched the deepest chords in their hearts. They loved to play and dance and sing. And laughter spilled from their souls. Now don't get me wrong, this bunch could scrap with one another just as vehemently as they could celebrate.

Across the Cimarron to the south, in what was and is known as Cheyenne Valley, stand the gleaming red peaks of the Gloss Mountains. One tall peak in particular, Lone Peak, was the subject of mysterious stories of Indians and cowboys. Every time we drove through Cheyenne Valley, Daddy would recount tales of long ago when Indians roamed the land. A book written by Robert E. King, 'Crossing the Cimarron at "21" Crossing' tells about a stone marker. Perhaps as recently as the early 1950's, it is believed Northwestern Oklahoma State University in Alva, Oklahoma dismantled the marker for purposes of study. That appears to be the last anyone knows about this sacred artifact of the Gloss Mountains. But I was blessed to have seen it standing faithfully atop the mountain.

The "21" Crossing over the Cimarron was Daddy's highway

to the world beyond the Webster Ranch. In about 1929, that highway seduced Daddy to travel all the way to California to soothe his lovelorn heart. But in a short year, he returned to his beloved Cheyenne Valley. As time passed, he moved out into the world but his love for family and the sanctity on the north of the crossing always beckoned him back over the sacred bridge.

Remember, there were two families depicted here. My father's family, the Websters, who lived on land previously occupied by the Cheyenne Indians. Their ranch was just east and a little south of the "21" Crossing.

The other was my mother's family, the Johnsons. They lived on the north and to the west of the "21" Crossing, more in the proximity of the Cherokee Strip. In 1899, Anderson Woodruff (aka A.W.) Johnson moved his family to a sand farm in northern Oklahoma. With a dugout for a home, the family began life in Indian Territory then called the Cherokee Strip. A.W. Johnson was my grandfather. Not long after his move, A.W.'s wife, Laura, died in childbirth. Grandfather was left the single parent of four children ranging in ages between eight and just under two years old.

Life was difficult. Feeding and clothing four children from the profits of the sand hills was not easy. In 1906, Grandfather put an ad in the Comfort Magazine with circulation in many surrounding states. The ad read, "Widower with four children needs companion."

Compelled by her love of children, Lenola Norman of Economy, Indiana answered the ad. She communicated with A.W. for a few months. Then in February of 1907, Lenola rode the train to Waynoka, Indian Territory (now Oklahoma) to become the mailorder bride of A.W. Johnson. She arrived with all her worldly possessions, her beautiful clothes, her collection of books, and her massive pump organ, all were a sign she planned to make good on her intentions to wed this stranger.

The train delivered her one day and she married A. W. Johnson the following day. Lenola had come from a well-to-do family, her father was the inventor of some part of the lawn mower. She had gone to Earlham School of Religion in Richmond, Indiana, then taught piano to young children.

After marrying Anderson Woodruff (A.W.) Johnson in Indian Territory, they moved into a small dugout in the side of a sand hill with newsprint on the walls for designer effects. Lenola spread the low ceilings above the children's beds with the 'funnies' so they would have something to read. And on October fifth, 1908, Lenola gave birth to a daughter named Irene Lenora Johnson. Lenola was my grandmother and Irene was my mother.

Before finishing high school, my mother, Irene, became a teacher. When she was sixteen her father, my grandfather, took her to Alva, Oklahoma to attend Normal School in hopes of training to become a teacher. They loaded in the spring wagon pulled by Dan and Bob, Grandpa's two gray horses, drove twenty miles to Alva, went house to house seeking a family willing to barter housing and meals in exchange for light housekeeping and child care duties. Mr. and Mrs. Carlin, kind friends of grandfather's oldest daughter, set strict expectations before agreeing to this arrangement.

Mother was grateful. It was compulsory that she pass a competency test. Those passing the Normal School test were granted certificates authorizing them to teach in one room elementary schools with all eight grades. The first year mother was hired to teach at Twin Oaks, a rural school near her family's farm. The following year mother's sister had acquired her teaching credentials. Mother decided to let her apply at Twin Oaks. In turn, Mother agreed to apply at Golden Valley, a school near the Webster Ranch. Prior to this, mother was not as familiar with the "21" Crossing as her Webster counterparts.

In 1893, Grandfather served as clerk of what was referred to as the Bilson School District #22, located in Greenwood County, Kenner, Kansas, a position he held continuously until the end of the 1902 school year. He was an advocate of education for the youngest in society. Then again, when the Websters moved to Indian Territory, he served on the Golden Valley School Board. When my mother, Irene, applied for a position at Golden Valley Grandfather was very impressed with her astute demeanor. She was hired soon after with one little hitch. Where would she live? As was customary, the school board was responsible for locating housing for the new school 'Marm.' With my father away in California, it was decided mother would stay with the Webster family.

Mother's mode of transportation was her bay pony. Every Sunday evening she would ride her pony to the Webster Ranch. And every Friday evening she would return to her family's farm north of the river. When the water level of the Cimarron rose, she would ride along the banks then cut through the low tide of the water to reach her destination. I can only imagine what that scene looked like.

Mother was a lighthearted young lady with shoulder length blond hair of bouncing curls induced by winding sections of her hair around rags. She was happy, studious, a good writer, enjoyed reading, and a person of integrity. With her guitar, she created her own version of music in the one room school. I can picture Friday afternoons after all her students struck out for home. More than likely, she would angle her guitar across her shoulder, toss a book bag over the neck of her pony, then leap on his back.

She was quick to learn how to navigate the river. One tantalizing request to her horse's flank and he would stretch out on a dead run toward her home north of the Cimarron. Mother was made of tough stuff when would-be calamities threatened to seduce her. I can still see the steel in her eyes as she bowed into the challenges of life in an effort to make lemonade to serve her adversaries. She lived with the spirit of a realist who risked with caution.

Then along came Dewey S. Webster, one whose spirit bounced around in the lives of his family, in musical lyrics, in farming, and in dreaming beyond anything he might ever know. He loved the 'what if's, the maybes, and the perhaps.' On occasion, when his back was against the wall of danger, he would challenge fate.

Two unlikely spirits melting together.

# Chapter Twenty-One

## O-SI-YO

    According to my Daddy, when he returned from California and discovered a sweet young teacher had taken up residence with his family, his lovelorn heart abandoned its disparity. In a matter of minutes, he picked up his violin and commenced to create a special tune for her. That was as far as he would venture with his part of the story but there was always a glint in his eye when he reminisced about her beautiful curls, her lovely pink dress, and her astute wisdom. He believed my Mother was the prettiest, the smartest, and the most faithful of any other woman.

    On the other hand, my Mother always felt inclined to pick up the story from there. In her diegesis of how the narrative went, she pointed to my Grandfather Marion Francis Webster I. Mother had grown to love the Websters, especially Grandfather Marion Francis. She did recognize favoritism when it was directed toward her. She described my Grandfather Marion Francis as soft spoken, respectful, kind, and with the spirit of a gracious gentleman. He was one who valued children, family, and education.

    Now, with regard to Irene, it seemed apparent he may have had a surreptitious motive. How often does one have a single son and a sweet young teacher living right there under his roof? Grandfather may have even crafted a few innocent schemes to encourage his recovering lovelorn single son to turn his attention toward Irene. After all, he believed she would make a good daughter-in-law. It wasn't long before Grandfather's cupid exploits toward Dewey and Irene gained momentum.

In the spring of 1930, Grandfather's health was in peril. By then, his efforts to bring these two together had struck a chord. The young couple announced the day they planned to marry. On that morning, July 27, 1930, it was apparent the veil was lifting for Grandfather to begin his journey toward the other side of life. He asked Dewey and Irene to come see him before going to the minister for the wedding ceremony.     Sometime   around one o'clock in the afternoon, Dewey donned his suit and Irene slipped into a sweet white lace ankle-length dress. When they arrived to see Grandfather, it was obvious he was growing weaker. He asked them to stand on chairs at the end of his bed so he could see how nice they looked together. A faint smile formed on his trembling lips as a warm tear meandered down his cheek. He was pleased.

Later that evening, Grandfather died. The mortician was notified. (In those days, the body was prepared and kept at home until the funeral.) Family and friends began to gather. It was summertime; the Webster home was too small to accommodate everyone. Those who chose to stay slept wherever they could find an empty spot be it the backseat of their car, the hay loft, or the trailer parked near the barn. This is the place in Mother's story where her voice lowers and she says with reverence, "We spent our honeymoon outside on the lawn near the house," meaning they slept on the grass. A few weeks after Grandfather's death, the children decided someone should stay with Grandmother Sarah Melinda. There were cattle to manage and crops to tend. Since Dewey and Irene were the only ones without little children, they seemed the obvious ones to care for Grandmother. Sarah Melinda lived on the ranch until the end of her days in 1934.

On the first anniversary of their marriage, Father went to Cleo Springs, Oklahoma for maintenance materials. Money was too short to purchase a gift for his beloved wife. He stopped by the Drugstore where all kinds of things were sold. As he searched up and down the aisles, he came upon a beautiful metal enameled box containing assorted chocolates. He had just barely enough money to purchase it.

Father hastened back to the ranch. It was July. It was hot. Chocolates would melt. No doubt Mother was surprised. She and my Father enjoyed the delicacies and kept the box as a treasure. Down through the years, that box became my Mother's safe where she stored important papers and small items. Now it graces a credenza in my home. These are spirits I hold dear to my heart.

Father was a barber and a farmer. In their early years of marriage, he bought barbershops in various small towns but finally settled in Chester, Oklahoma. By that time, he and my mother had four tots. Since family was important to both of them, they vowed to see as much of their extended families as possible. From Chester, the way back to their childhood homes near the Valley of the Cheyenne was over the "21" Crossing. But on this day, in the spring of 1945, our trip back across the river had a different purpose.

# Chapter Twenty-Two

## O-SI-YO

    Six-year-old cousin Lowell lived on the north side of the historical Cimarron River. He begged to spend the week with our family on the south of the river. His visit had come to an end and, as promised, we were taking him home. It was 1945, the Second World War was raging in Europe, and motor fuel and automobile tires rationed. The 21 Crossing over the Cimarron was the shortest route from our home to his. In my young lifetime, we had made this trip many times to visit grandparents. When we could see the 'Old 21' bridge we knew we were getting close to family. But on this day that followed the down pouring of spring rains, we were met with unexpected challenges.

    Torrential rains had fallen for several days, the ground was soaked, bar ditches were overflowing, and the river was swollen with muddy waters. In the early '40's many rural roads were not hard surfaced. Tire friction and heavy rains would churn the soil into red mud making travel difficult and hazardous. With a great deal of stress and angst, we made our way through the Gloss Mountains of Cheyenne Valley and turned north toward the Cimarron Crossing slipping and sliding through the murky gumbo. Thick red water sloshed up through what was left of the floorboards in our old '33 Ford.

On this particular Sunday, in 1945, the river had become a raging, tempestuous, wrathful, vicious, body of water. Streams of golden sunlight bounced on the rushing muddy waters as the power of the mighty Cimarron surged against the bridge known as the 'Old 21.' It creaked and swayed and twisted against the charging fury of the river.

When Daddy rounded the corner approaching the bridge, he could see ahead the rolling of the river out of its banks. He inched the car closer. Then stopped. "What's wrong, Dewey?" Mother asked. "I think the '21' is out," Daddy answered. He took the car out of gear while he surveyed the fateful scene. Daddy continued, "The rain has washed part of the bridge away."

And sure enough, as we looked closer, the wooden planks that formed the abutment approach to the "21" Crossing were gone. We could see some of them as they were bantered about along the south edge of the Cimarron. Daddy stood on the running board of the car to get a better look. His further inspection revealed gaping holes in the entirety of the half-mile bridge.

It was late afternoon. And at best there was barely time enough for us to take Lowell home and then return to ours. Turning around to take the long route to his house, struggling through more mud-slogged roads, gambling on thread bare tires, limited fuel, and impending darkness was more than Daddy could handle.

In disbelief that the "21" Crossing was about to succumb to the powerful turbulence of the Cimarron, daddy pondered our options for confronting the mighty raging red waters of the Cimarron. As I am trying to recapture the essence of this scene, I am reminded of a biblical event involving a sea of red waters holding a group of people hostage. Moses must have had some of the same helpless feelings as my daddy. Well, even Moses couldn't change the impossible into a possibility without a little divine assistance. Nor could daddy. Armed with faith, confidence, and determination, he began shaping his plan.

Parts of the south abutment were sloshing about near the approach to the bridge. Daddy knew it would be necessary to try to restore his old friend to a useful state. Defeat at the hands of Mother Nature was diametric and difficult for his determined spirit to accept.

Daddy considered the muddy roads, the partially washed-out bridge, and the child whose anticipation of seeing his family bore deep. With caution he opened the car door, placed his size twelve shoes in the squishy mud, and began to gather planks from the destruction of the bridge. After mulling over the possibilities, he placed the boards strategically to create tracks the exact width of the wheels on the car. "Now, Mother, you take the children and walk across the bridge. I am going to drive the car up these tracks to the bridge and I'll meet you on the other side." Even as a young child, I wondered what that might mean when he said 'the other side.' The other side of the bridge? Or the other side after life?

I think if it were possible for me to rummage through the archives of terror imprinted upon my life, this event would be the crown to top all others. And with it, I'd find a child's angst-ridden query of Daddy's plan. It would probably go something like this:

"What do you mean get out of the car? In this muck and mud? You can't be serious! And we're gonna walk over that bridge that is about to abandon its purpose and go with the wild torrents of the river? I don't think so.

Oh, but we are. Daddy said for us to.
Surely he'll change his mind.
Nope, we're really gonna do this.
Oh, help us!"

The furrows on mother's forehead deepened as she said, "Oh, Dewey, I'm afraid for you to do that. You might go off the tracks and into the river."

"I'll take it slow and I'll be careful. You take the children on ahead. I'll see you on the other side of the bridge."

Mother helped each of us up the tracks to the top of the bridge—the bridge now weakened by the stress of the rushing waters and one that could wash downstream any moment.

"Momma, when I look down I can see the water in the river splashing on the bottom of the bridge," I cried. As she led the way Momma looked side to side at each of us to make sure we were safe. "Oh if I'm not careful I might fall through one of these holes.

I'm scared, Momma," I thought.

"Be careful," she cautioned. "Watch your step and hurry along. We'll be on the other side soon. Daddy is going to drive the car across."

The following day remnants of the "21" Crossing broke loose and traveled with the unruly current downstream never again to be a crossing over the Cimarron. We were the last to caress the fragile wooden planks that had once borne the traf-fic of the northwest.

When I pull this day from my memory, I see two young girls in feed sack dresses, shoes run over at the sides, socks drooped loosely above the ankles; three boys with overalls long since out grown, heavy boots with polish that had made little difference, and a faithful and courageous mother shepherding her children to safety. With rigid stalk-like bodies anchored by wobbly weak knees, they trudged through a tortuous trauma.

Following this foot parade, in a 1933 Ford sedan, was one gutsy and determined young man who made the choice to challenge the disaster of the fearsome river. It was only when daddy took his foot off the brakes and allowed the car to roll gently off the exit ramp of the bridge, I knew we were safe. As much as I was scared when daddy told us his plan for tackling the assault on the bridge, I believed in his inviolability to orchestrate it with fervor. Every child has faith in his parents ability to keep him safe. At that moment, he was bigger than life to me. Something stronger than fear, carried us across the treacherous "21" Crossing that day—a day when faith and fear walked hand in hand.

# Chapter Twenty-Three

## O-SI-YO

This is the story of a person whose spirit continues to inspire my life. Even though she was not a part of my family her presence resides with me. I honor her. I respect who she was. I will always remember her. There was a certain holiness and innate goodness about her.

It is true that teachers anoint children with a part of themselves and leave lifelong impressions scattered upon those whose lives they touch. Thus it is that children become the Keepers of those impressions. My second grade teacher, Sadie Lawton, and I entered into a three year partnership that indelibly colored both our lives.

Sadie's quiet and reticent manner invited the same from this wriggly and boisterous seven year old girl. Sadie was slight in stature. Her head was crowned with flocks of chemically induced dark auburn hair, fine in texture, and whimsical by nature. It was coiffed in neat waves that began at the top of her head and continued down the back and sides. When not in the classroom, a perky hat accentuated the tight curls framing her face and neck. Sadie's eyes matched the color of her hair. I don't remember her expressing favored affection toward any one child. All were given special attention. Her steady, glistening, and sometimes mischievous eyes spoke of her warm feelings for children. Evidenced by the vibrations of her head, a mild affliction of palsy possessed her body.

Sadie may have been in her mid forties. She had taught at Garden Vale (isn't that a wonderful name for a primary school?) a few years before I entered second grade. It is well known that teachers of young children leave lasting imprints on their students. My penchant for becoming a teacher may be somewhat rooted in Sadie's tenderhearted spirit.

Sadie never owned a car. In the distance, the labored chugging and clattering of Sam's old red pickup announced that it was headed in the direction of the one room country school near Chester, a quiet village in northwest Oklahoma. It groaned its complaints as it struggled to pull Sadie's 1935 UTC (unidentified travel coach aka as an early rendition of a mobile home) on to the grounds of the school.

Sadie had signed on to be the teacher of Garden Vale. Since it was a country school, Sadie was responsible for securing temporary living arrangements. Every year her brother, Sam, would dutifully reposition her tiny home on wheels. With surgical precision, he would nestle the travel trailer between the school and the coal shed. It was a place of choice that provided protection from the erratic weather of northwest Oklahoma and was in close proximity to the comfort facilities down a crooked path behind the trailer. An in-ground fresh water pump near the portico of the school waited to accommodate her needs. Inside the portico a long rope attached to a huge bell above, hung in silence awaiting the draw that would order the call to gather.

Sadie's travel trailer was approximately eight feet by twelve feet. It was complete with a kitchenette, a minimal sitting area, and a space with a full size bed. She shared this living arrangement with her mother, Helen. Kerosene fueled the lamp that pierced the darkness and the heater that took the chill out of the air when temperatures dropped. The space may have been somewhat confining but it satisfied Sadie and Helen's needs.

Sadie had never married. To facilitate the occasional moves from one school to another they lived in this very (very) small trailer home. It was somewhat on the order of the tiny homes now touted on television for those who want to have a place to hang their hat without the exorbitant financial investment. Some of those are a mere 300 square feet. Sadie's small trailer was even tinier than that. Each time Sadie accepted a teaching position she pulled her little home on wheels onto the grounds of the school where she would live until her tenure expired. I'm not sure how all this worked for the two of them but it was absolutely marvelous for all of us who were under her tutelage. Her mother served as counselor, tutor, nurse, and comforter.

When Sadie accepted the position at Garden Vale she set up residence in her tiny trailer not far from the door of the school house. That year there were thirty-nine students in the school. Eight of those thirty-nine were in the second grade. With the wide range of academic requirements, it was difficult for Sadie to be engaged with every student for extended periods. While she worked with the greater number of children in the school, her mother assumed a supportive role. So we were privileged to be in a two-for-one salary situation.

Incidentally, salaries for teachers then were somewhere between seventy-five and one hundred dollars per month. Many times they were given a promissory note (a promise to pay the teacher when the school district got the money). Sometimes small town grocery stores would honor these notes so people could purchase food. On Saturday afternoons, Sadie could be seen walking the one mile over a sandy road to town for groceries. She would be clad in a prim dress, two inch high heeled shoes, black stockings, a dainty black purse, all adorned with a perky hat on top of her head. After shopping for her weekly groceries and preparing to pay the clerk, she would open the clasp of her purse, turn its contents out on top of the counter and begin counting enough coins to make her payment.

After Sadie finished working with each class, they were given exclusive tasks and privileges, often this meant they could visit Grandma Helen in the little house on wheels. She was sure to read or tell them a story. On the other hand, if someone had difficulty with his/her facts (addition, subtraction, multiplication or division), reading lesson, spelling words, or geography assignment, they were sure to be sent to the little trailer to work under the loving tutelage of Grandma Helen.

Most likely she would offer a treat as a bonus for hard work or just because you were you. These treats came in the form of cookies, cakes, candies, and trinkets of all kinds. The most treasured treat was a miniature paper parasol. I would have washed blackboards for a week to receive just one of those little pink or blue umbrellas with a canopy that really raised and collapsed. (Sometimes life is like one of those little umbrellas, it goes up and down yet all the while there is a cover overhead protecting from adverse conditions.)

Sadie was one of those rare teachers who believed in going heavy on the positive and light on the negative as a means of encouraging children to do their best. She was consistent and predictable. Let me make it clear right here and now. Sadie was no push over. I do not want to leave the impression that Sadie operated out of an understanding that children only do well when motivated with some tangible item. Sadie loved children. She believed in surprises, magic, and fun. Her gifts were tokens of those. Sadie received more from children's smiles than from their puzzlement. She seemed to know that it was important for children to experience more successes than defeats and she set about creating an environment in which that could happen. On occasion when recess was called, Sadie could be seen standing at bat, then 'running the bases' as the children cheered her on to the finish. (In her two inch high heeled shoes, no less.) Today, after more than thirty years of teaching young children, I am convinced Sadie was generations ahead of her time.

Remnants of her tender spirit live on through me. It might be said that I have become one (there are many) of the Keepers of Sadie's beautiful, pioneering spirit. Keepers are like ghosts who make holy that which is remembered within the soul and spirit of another. Another way of discussing the image of Ghosts as Keepers of the Spirits might be in the cartoon character of Casper the Friendly Ghost. The long trailing ethereal vapor might be representative of the spirits of all those each of us carries.

This is not to trivialize the images of the spirit but to paint a metaphor that symbolizes their embodiment of reality. A faint whisper can spark the quest to remember (to reassemble) fond remembrances and significant happenings surrounding another's life. It is stories of those who've gone on ahead that empower the generations that follow to dream and create. They lie in the fertile life soil that gives birth to the magic found in the surprises of life. Their residuum is the foundation laid down by those 'on whose shoulders we stand.' It invokes the courage to throw one's hat over the wall, so to speak, and step outside the conventional norm of life's expectations. It takes only an occasional phantom nudge of a well-meaning 'ghost' to seduce others to either sit it out, or to join in the dance of life.

    I am a committed 'Keeper of the Spirit' of Sadie and many others whose stories live on through me.

# Chapter Twenty-Four

## OH-SI-YO

In continuation of my quest to shed light on the story that consumes this writing, a few years ago I went to Tahlequah, Oklahoma, the home of the Cherokee Nation, to search for answers to my questions about the Cherokee maiden riding through the mountains of Tennessee or Illinois or wherever it was believed she was traveling. This was the "X" factor driving the story my father and his siblings vehemently carried with them into my future.

As a young child I was prone to think perhaps it was a contrived story. Now after gathering the bits and pieces, I believe there is a simple explanation. Some might say that my simple rationale should be enough. I believe I owe it to my readers to provide all the information I have gathered in making my case for a legitimate conclusion to this story.

The gentleman at the Cherokee Research Center in Tahlequah said for all practical purposes it could be a real possibility there is truth in the legend that makes all of us in the Webster family part Cherokee. It appears the Cherokee and other tribes as well made a concerted effort to adopt the ways of the white man. They assumed his culture, his dress, his lifestyle. To the extent, they approved the intermarriage of the races. There were claims that people by the name of Walker intermarried with the Eastern Cherokee Indians. Margaret Walker (1759-1842) Bedford, Virginia married John Richard Webster, (1759-1833) Amherst, Virginia, my third great grandfather.

The story of the Indian Maiden has remained a mystery. Nevertheless, it has steeped through the fiber of who I am and I embrace its' obscure implications. Here is my best effort to pass on the flavor of the story as it was told to me.

"Smoke from the tribal fires filled her nostrils. Her paint pony paced to the cadence of the tribal drums resounding through the mountains. She was dressed in buckskin matching her smooth and tender young skin. Her long black hair pulled away from her face; shaped in a strong braid that hung down her back. It was ornamented with feathers of the black hawk identifying her as one of the Cherokee Native American Indian Tribe. The braid swayed rhythmically with the side to side movement of her horse. Strapped to her back was a papoose cradling an infant. She had no provisions, only herself and the child."

Maybe I embrace her because the strength of her spirit represents who I'd like to be. Courageous and brave. Or still, it may be as simple as she was given to our family by the angels of those who've gone on before us and we are expected to lay claim over her. A mere gift to enjoy and to spark the passions of our imaginations. At any rate, I claim her wherever she was and whoever she was. One thing for certain she was, and is, of the Native American descent.

George Washington Webster II and Sidney Widger Webster were my great grandparents. They had a niece, Sarah Jane Webster, whose parents were deceased. For whatever reasons, Sarah Jane needed help caring for her new baby, Sarah Melinda Smith. Sidney Widger Webster and George Washington Webster II, Sarah Jane's aunt and uncle, stepped up to help care for Sarah Melinda.

Sarah Jane's aunt, Sidney Widger, would ride her horse along the trails of the Great Smoky Mountains to the home of Dr. Mimson (as previously alluded), bundle Sarah Melinda in a papoose, place her on her back, and return to her home with George Washington Webster II. This aunt cared for Sarah Melinda for several weeks, returning her to Sarah Jane for brief periods, then repeating her ride through the woods. When Sarah Melinda was sixteen years old she made the decision to claim her home with her aunt and uncle, Sidney and George Washington Webster. Sidney and George had eleven children, one of whom was Marion Francis Webster I. He was seventeen years old. Sarah Melinda and Marion Francis I had grown up together. When they came of age they married. They were my grandparents. Yes, they were cousins. Cousin married cousin. That may have been more acceptable in the 1800's than it would be today.

Sidney Widger, my great grandmother, was the Indian Maiden seen riding in and around the mountain trails lined with tall ash, white cedar, red oak, weeping willow, and flowering dogwood. She was carrying my grandmother Sarah Melinda Smith Webster.

# Chapter Twenty-Five

O-SI-YO

    Now to the end of my story, the X Factor, the Cherokee Maiden. First, I want to establish what I believe to be a reminiscent culmination of Native American DNA in our Webster family lineage. I haven't checked this evidence with Scotland Yard, but my investigations lead me to a couple of analogies that point to distinct Native American DNA in our Webster family. Given the fact, that such spans several generations, the bloodline runs thin but it connects, and that is all that matters.

### Analogy # One

    The Indian connection is noted through the Widger family line. Widger sisters married Webster brothers—Francis Marion Webster I and George Washington Webster II. Sidney Widger was my great grandmother. She was married to George Washington Webster II. Sidney Widger's grandfather, William Widger, my third great grandfather was married to Elizabeth Dove who was of the Mississippi Choctaw Tribe thereby Sidney Widger was of Native American descent.

## Analogy # Two

I found an article that discussed the likelihood that the Cherokee Walker family intentionally intermarried with the Webster Family. According to the administrator of genealogical research at the Cherokee Tribal headquarters in Tahlequah, Oklahoma, many Native Americans were eager to assume the ways of the white man - his dress - his farming skills - his social attitudes? So quite possibly this is what happened in our Webster family. Margaret Walker of Bedford, Virginia married John Richard Webster Sr., my third great grandfather. Margaret was of the Cherokee Tribe. If that be true, then that is another way our Webster family could be considered of Native American descent.

Another little factor that has been revealed in the last few years is that of a Lost Tribe. According to one news source, when the tribe set out on the Trail of Tears a faction of the Cherokee Tribe broke loose perhaps somewhere near Illinois. They traveled incognito into Arkansas and hid out in the shelter of caves and blackjack trees. They feared prosecution, if found by the United States Government. Some believe there are those who are still intimidated by this dark shadow that lurks in the history of the Cherokee Nation. The journey our Webster family made from Tennessee was long and tedious. When they became so weary they couldn't go any further, they put down roots in the Chicago, Illinois area. Then several years later they moved on to Kansas. It is plausible to conjure a belief that some could have struck out with the faction that fled into Arkansas and were presumed lost for a great number of years. One report was that ancestors that separated from the Cherokee Nation and settled in the states of Arkansas, Kansas, Missouri, and Texas lost their citizenship in the Cherokee Nation. Perhaps that is the reason our Webster family could not be traced through the Dawes Rolls of Native American Registry.

When I went to Tahlequah, Oklahoma, the home of the Cherokee Nation, to search for answers to my questions about the Cherokee maiden riding through the mountains of Tennessee or Illinois or wherever she planned or hoped or believed her journey would take her. This was the "X" factor driving the story my father and his siblings vehemently carried with them into my future. Now I've come to believe there is a simple explanation and I believe that what I allege is true.

# Chapter Twenty-Six

*O-SI-YO*

To conclude this query—it appears we are both Choctaw and Cherokee. The child being carried by the Indian Maiden was Sarah Melinda Smith Webster, daughter of Sarah Jane Webster Smith, my paternal great grandmother. The haze that clouded the "X" factor has been lifted. No need to puncture your finger with a black crow's calamus for blood in a unity ceremony. That blood thing happened long ago when our great great grandmother Elizabeth Hubbard left her home in the hills of Tennessee to unite with a family of English/Welsh/Native American descent. Now we are free to claim a tribal heritage. From this day forward, the wonder and magic surrounding the mystery of the legend will remain dear to my heart.

It is my suspicion that most everyone born in Oklahoma has Native American DNA of one tribe or another.

# Chapter Twenty-Seven

*O-SI-YO*

Well, not so fast. This story will never end because I, the Spirit Keeper, hold the mystery of beautiful spirits in trust. They are only a whisper away. Like money in the bank, you can withdraw from wonder and magic all that you need to satisfy the yearnings of your heart. I will never know all the details of authenticity that credit this story. No one knows another's inner thoughts and passions. Nevertheless, the story as has been recounted has held me in its clutches. I embrace the hazy glow of its' intrinsic merit. Here is my best effort to pass on the flavor of the story as it was told to me.

Smoke from the tribal fires filled her nostrils. Her pinto pony paced to the cadence of the tribal drums resounding through the mountains. Dressed in buckskin matching her smooth and tender young skin. Her long black hair pulled away from her face; shaped in a strong braid that hung down her back. It was ornamented with feathers of the black hawk identifying her as one of the Choctaw Native American Indian Tribe. The braid swayed rhythmically with the clip clop of hooves and side to side adjustment of her steed. Strapped to her back was a papoose cradling an infant. She had no provisions, only herself and the child. As related before, these were my great grandmother Sidney Widger and my grand-mother Sarah Melinda Webster.

Now more than ever before, it seems obvious some details may have been lost in the recalling and the re-telling of this story. What I do know is that in 1830, the political atmosphere of the nation was governed by President Andrew Jackson. He invoked the Indian Removal Act of 1830 that forced Native Americans to surrender their lands claimed and inhabited long before the white man arrived on the scene. It was a brash and deceitful governmental manipulation. They were being forced to leave their home in the beautiful Smoky Mountains of Tennessee. In exchange for their land, The Five Civilized Tribes were promised a new land of their own. The problem with this arrangement was that the new land was halfway across the United States. It was called Indian Territory, Oklahoma.

What the government didn't tell these quiet, peaceful people was they would have to scrounge for a way to get to the new land. Walk, go on horseback, ride in a wagon, or paddle a canoe. The raucous message of the government was that they didn't care just so long as they were gone from Tennessee, South and North Carolina, and Georgia. A good share of the Cherokees had lived on the Qualla Indian Reservation in Tennessee all their lives. Large bands of Indians set off on foot to reach their new home in Oklahoma. More than 4,000 died from exposure, disease, and various causes.

This was the Trail of Tears. This was one of the many narratives that chronicled Sidney Ellen Widger's life. She was the Indian Maiden who lived in the shadows of this shameful event that ignited an eternal flame in the pages of Oklahoma History. Her presence crossed the invisible boundaries of ethnicities. Now her stalwart spirit continues to influence the evolution of a nation in its struggle to become aligned with that which is honorable, that which is moral, and that which is just. This is her story. This is her history.

One thing is certain, this story has given our family the impetus for digging through the archives of our lives intent on discovering who we are. It is a romantic love story tweaking the spirits of our past, rattling the cage of our present, and opening the doors to new identities for all of us. This of itself presents a viable case for the justification, if such is needed, of my passion to lean as close as possible to the spirit of Sidney Ellen Widger Webster. She represents much of who I'd like to be. Courageous, brave, stalwart. It would make me happy to peek through the pages of time at what destiny brought her into our family. But for now, that will remain a secret sealed within her heart. I will rejoice in what I have discovered and live in the warm blessing of her spirit.

Our stories add richness to our lives and to the lives of others. Share the legends, myths, and stories of your family and friends with neighbors, with the clerk in the grocery, with the President, with anyone who will stand still long enough to listen. Your stories coupled with those of others become the springboard for keeping the spirits of ones we hold dear alive. In this technological age, it is easy to confuse symbolic text messaging with direct verbal communicating with friends. Symbolic is just what it implies — black, white, one letter or syllable interaction. In no way, does it capture the essence of the spirit of the sender nor the recipient. Each of us is a Keeper of the Spirits and Myths of those in our present and our past. Look into the eyes of each other and share your stories. Treasure them. Hold them in reference and be grateful they blessed you with their presence. This is your Spiritual Journey. Enjoy it.

This is my story. This is our story. It is not a fable nor an epic folk tale or a myth. It is a true legend of a luminary nature surrounding the sacred spirits of persons in our family.

Like a shining light you will live on in my heart. I am the Keeper of Spirits and I will keep your spirit safe and in the company of the saints who have gone before us. It is my hope you will share this story with your children and all other generations to come.
"To You And To All You Hold Dear."
Namaste

Sidney Ellen Widger Webster, the Indian Maiden, of the Mississippi Choctaw Tribe once the "X" factor of our Webster family. Now known as the one who carried Sarah Melinda Smith Webster to and from visiting her mother. Sarah Melinda's mother Sarah Jane Webster Smith had a difficult life. Lost both parents when she was young, married at age fourteen, went to work, had her first child at sixteen, absent husband until he surfaced in 1865 when he volunteered in the Union Army with the 61st Cavalry Regiment, was reported deceased in 1869. Sarah Jane married again several years later to a man who was harsh and unkind to her infant daughter, Sarah Melinda Smith. Sarah Jane sacrificed her early mothering years with her daughter Sarah Melinda by sending her to a safe place to live with her great uncle and aunt, George Washington Webster II and Sidney Ellen Widger Webster. Sarah Jane's reward: Her daughter Sarah Melinda Smith Webster (my grandmother), married my grandfather Marion Francis Webster I who loved and cared for her till the end of her time. Sidney Ellen Widger Webster was my paternal great grandmother. I am blessed by her Native American spirit.

Sidney Ellen Widger Webster

# Chapter Twenty-Eight

O-SI-YO

In the end...

...my initial dilemma was to make the distinction between fable and fiction, legend and folklore, and myth or truth surrounding a story told by my father and his siblings. On my journey to solve the case surrounding the mysterious Indian Maiden carrying an infant as she rode her sleek buckskin pony through the mountains of eastern Illinois, I declared to you my readers that I did not know what I would do if I was not able to uncover her identity. Nor did I know what I would do if I did discover who she was, where she came from, and what she was doing. After intense research and gleanings from members of the Webster family, the curtain has been lifted; the mystery has been unraveled. Daddy was right. Sarah Melinda Smith, my grandmother, was the child Sidney Ellen Widger carried in the papoose on her back as she rode along the winsome mountain trails.

I now declare Sidney Ellen Widger Webster the unmasked X factor subject of my search. My family believed her to be my great grandmother. And she was. With logic and specificity, I hereby proclaim Sidney Ellen Widger Webster of the Mississippi Choctaw Indian Tribe to be one and the same.

What will I do now that I have discovered the truth of my dilemma? I will celebrate the Charm of the Spirit Keeper.

Aye, ye, ye, ye. Aye, ye, ye, ye. I hear the spirit of my grandfather Marion Francis Webster I, drummer of his Tribe, replicating the hushed rhythm of the delicate scissortail flycatcher in his flight searching for a place to pause. Or, perhaps it is the muffled tenor of the placid morning dove. Or could it be the sharp, crisp call of the scarlet red eastern cardinal darting among the berries of the holly. Oh, and here comes the graceful eagle in flight. The meter gathers speed and calls all to enter the dance of spirits near and far away. Grandfather boosts the tempo, feet hasten to the challenge, voices lift their supplications to the God of the Heavens and the God of the Earth. One God, the same. Prayers of praise kindle the fire that brings to life the joyful songs of the spirits who have brought us thus far.

Joyful. joyful we adore thee. God of glory. Lord of love. Hearts unfold like flowers before thee opening to the sun above. Melt the clouds of sin and sadness. Drive the dark of doubt away. Giver of immortal gladness. Fill us with the light of day.

The beat of the drum now indistinct. Movement stifled. Heads bowed in reverence. Spirits emerge from wispy veils. Dancers retreat within reflective hearts. Souls in communion. In the stillness, a solemn chant gives rise to a shining Light over taking the darkness. And Peace rests upon them.

Gracious and Loving Lord,
Thank you for creating each one of us in the image of your son, Christ Jesus.
You have marked us with the sign of His Cross and claimed us as your own.
Draw us into Your Light.
Restore in us your spirit of Love
That we might become all that you have created us to be.
It is in the name of the Father, The Son, and the Holy Spirit.
Amen

- Prayer of the Spirit Keeper -

# ACKNOWLEDGMENTS

It is not possible to write a family centered story without the collaboration of others. Family and friends have been patient listening to my renderings and rantings. They have urged and assisted me in compiling the historical recordings of the Webster family journey. I believe collective personal remembrances fortify the validity of any story. To those brave spirits who were willing to take a look back at the road traveled, please accept my humble gratitude.

I am grateful to those saints who continue to encourage me to explore the precipice of my place in time. With their gentle coaxing, the silhouette of my journey is defined by those on whose shoulders I stand. With their blessings, I will live out my dreams in the shelter of that power greater than myself.

Special thanks go to my dear sweet husband Larry L. Miles who has edited and re-edited the words written here. He has put on the garments of patience and kindness as I have pushed him beyond reason. It is a mystery to me that I should be so blessed to be making this journey through life with him. Thank you, God.

# PERMISSIONS

Page 13, photo, Gloss Mountains, photographer, Stiddon Sikes

Page 26, Cone Marker-Indian Medicine Wheel, Northwestern University (1-580-327-1700)

Page 29, map, Trail of Tears, U.S. National Park Service, (1-918-453-500), granted by Head of Research department

Page 34, Map of Indian Territories of Oklahoma, Oklahoma Historical Society, Patricia Jones (1-405-522-4025)

Page 38, map, Quallah Boundary, Home of the Eastern Cherokee Indians, Photo by: Kevin Brocious, 828.553.0749

Page 113, Aerial photo of Webster Ranch

"There is a reason you are here in this time and in this place.
Ponder who you are, whose you are, and who you hope to become."

"It is when you have the courage to draw strength and wisdom from reflections of the past that you can bask in the joy of today and prepare for the challenges of tomorrow."

All Are Spirit Keepers Of All That Is
Just as the moon is the 'Keeper of' light in any particular time and place, are you the Keeper of God in your particular time and place? When you realize God's Holy presence in yourself you must be cognizant of His presence in others. Go forth to all corners of the earth and spread the 'good news' that God is With Us now and forever more.

- SAMANTHA NORMAN -

The Spirit Keeper

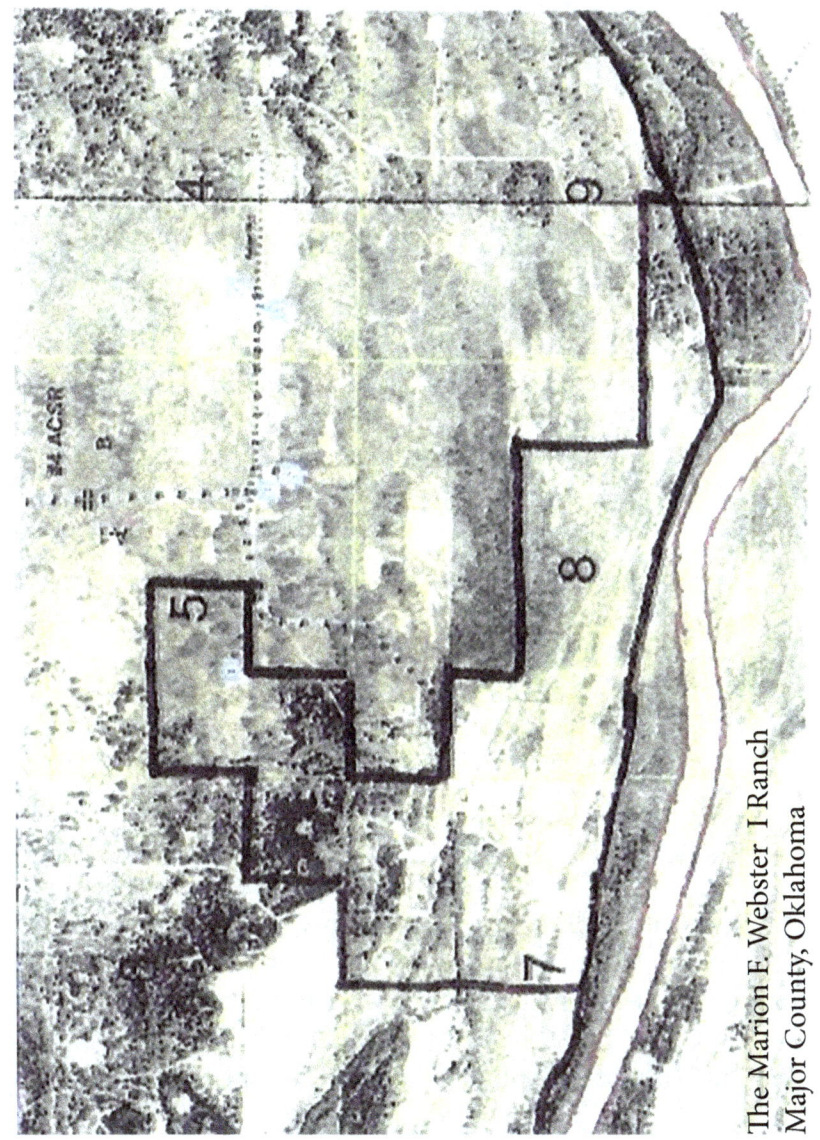

The Marion F. Webster I Ranch
Major County, Oklahoma

## ABOUT THE AUTHOR

DONNA N. MILES considers herself a writer committed to preserving the history, as she knows it, of her family. Be it a skilled or apprentice writer is of little significance when sharing the unique scripts of your life. Donna delights in her mission to gift others with a glimpse of the treasures held dear to her and her tribal family. She invites others to do the same. It is in the sharing that we find meaning and grow in love of one another.

In 2012, Donna penned and published her first book titled **Running Without A Soul**. It is her sincere hope that **Charmed By The Spirit Keeper** will warm your heart.

Miss Lily, one very independent lynx point cat, allows Donna and husband Larry to share her home in Edmond, Oklahoma.

www.ingramcontent.com/pod-product-compliance
Lightning Source LLC
Chambersburg PA
CBHW052100070526
44584CB00017B/2269